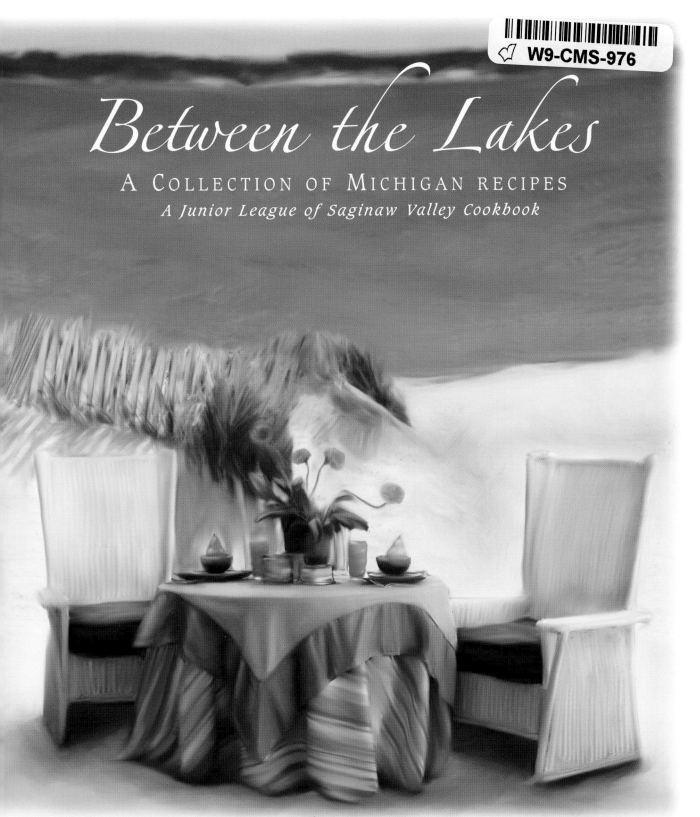

Between the Lakes

A COLLECTION OF MICHIGAN RECIPES

A Junior League of Saginaw Valley Cookbook

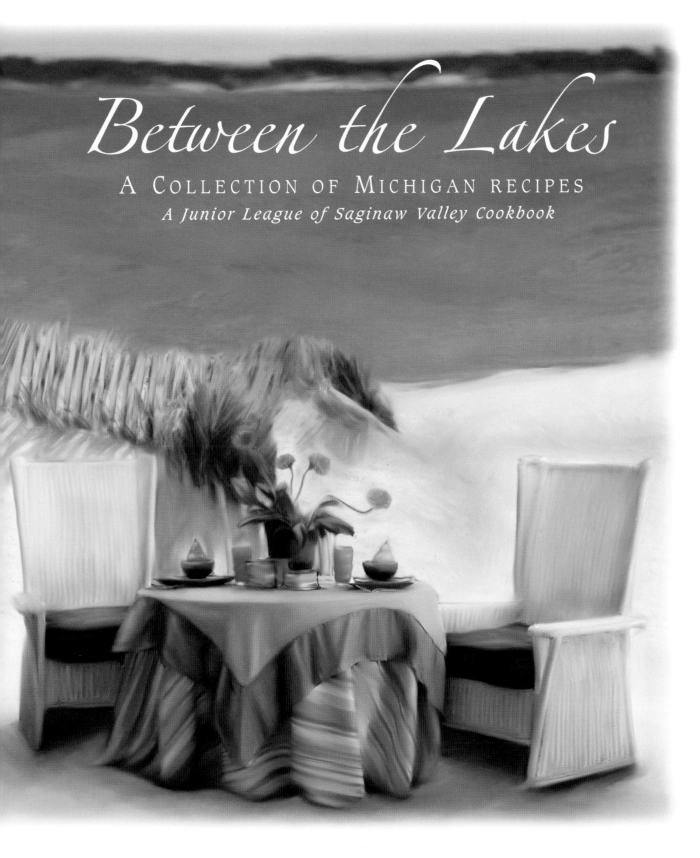

Between the Lakes

A COLLECTION OF MICHIGAN RECIPES

A Junior League of Saginaw Valley Cookbook

Between the Lakes

A Collection of Michigan Recipes

Published by
Junior League of Saginaw Valley

Copyright © 2005 by
Junior League of Saginaw Valley
5228 State Street
Saginaw,
Michigan 48603
989-790-3763

This cookbook is a
collection of favorite recipes,
which are not necessarily
original recipes.

Library of Congress Card Number: 2004105756
ISBN-10: 0-9752691-0-0
ISBN-13: 978-0-9752691-0-7

Edited, Designed, and Manufactured by
Favorite Recipes® Press
An imprint of

FRP™

P.O. Box 305142
Nashville, Tennessee 37230
800-358-0560

Art Director: Steve Newman
Book Design: Brad Whitfield and
    Susan Breining
Project Editor: Linda Jones

Manufactured in the United States of America
First Printing: 2005   6,000 copies
Second Printing: 2006   6,000 copies

Introduction

Between the Lakes *is a delightful collection of culinary surprises brought to you by the great state of Michigan and the Junior League of Saginaw Valley. The name Michigan is derived from the Algonquian word* michigama, *meaning "big water" or "great lake." Michigan has more than 11,000 lakes. Michigan's fertile soils, temperate climate, and abundant farmland make it a perfect location for the harvest of many fruits, vegetables, meats, and other products. Many people are aware that Traverse City, Michigan, is the "Cherry Capital of the World," but few realize that Michigan is a national leader in the production of blueberries, beans, peaches, and celery.*

As you circle around our beautiful state, you are struck by its unparalleled beauty and an amazing array of natural resources. In the southwest corner of the state, you will find the quaint lakeside towns of New Buffalo and Saugatuck, as well as the picturesque Warren Sand Dunes. Nearby are orchards rich in fruit, vineyards full of flavor, and vegetable farms that produce celery, asparagus, snap beans, and carrots. Farther up the western coastline, you pass through Holland with its magnificent floral wealth. Continuing along Lake Michigan, speckled with famous lighthouses, you come upon the Leelanau Peninsula, lush with sweet and tart cherry trees, and the old fishing town of Leland, a prime location to catch lake or brown trout, Chinook or coho salmon. Crossing the majestic Mackinac Bridge between Lake Michigan and Lake Huron, you enter the rugged wilderness of Michigan's Upper Peninsula. Sportsmen cherish this area for its plentiful deer, partridge, and wild turkey. This region's forests overflow with maple syrup. Returning to the Lower Peninsula along the eastern shoreline through the coastal towns of Cheboygan, Alpena, and Tawas, you eventually find yourself in the Saginaw Valley approaching the "Thumb of the Mitten." This area contains the richest farmland in the state, producing corn, dry beans, potatoes, and sugar beets. Completing the tour of our state along the St. Clair River near the Detroit area, you will see an abundance of waterfowl, including many varieties of ducks and geese.

Take time to enjoy our great state; visit Tahquamenon Falls with a friend, roll on the Sleeping Bear Dunes with a child, or hunt for Petoskey stones on Little Traverse Bay. Picnic at the Pictured Rocks on Lake Superior or create a gourmet meal to enjoy on a sunset sail across Saginaw Bay, using one of the delicious recipes from this book.

We hope you enjoy your journey Between the Lakes!

Great Lakes Sponsors

JUNIOR LEAGUE OF SAGINAW VALLEY SUSTAINERS

Mary Ahrens
Kathryn Moss Baumgarten
Mary Ann Beird
Jane Bommarito
Nancy Bow
Darlene Bry
Octavia Cabey
Margaret Clark
Carol Coppage
Culli Damuth
Janet Day
Karen Demetriou
Susan Dikeman
Corrine Dill
Sandy Donahue
Jeanne Draper
Dixie Drinan
Diane Ederer
Julia Emede
Barb Ewend
Jody Farley
Linda Fettig
Anne Flegenheimer
Dorothy Foulds
Veronica Furlo
Mary Goedert
Robin Greene
Catherin Hall
Vera Hanisko
Constance Harvey
Kathleen M. Heyn
Marcia Hoffman
Melanie Hollman
Laura Humphreys

Pamala Jarema
Carol Johnson
Martha Ann Joseph
Jane Jurgens
Sara Jury
Sharon Kaylor
Elizabeth Kelly
Sheryl Kendrick
Pam King
Caroline Knowlton
Nancy Koepke
Cyndy Lange
Patricia Learman
Josephine Lee
Margaret Lennon
Peggy Lotridge
Nancy MacRae
Virginia McCullough
Joanne Mcleod
Roslyn McQueen
Patricia Michalski
Sandra Morford
Kathy Morley
Marge Mulholland
Susie Nielsen
Georgia Northway
Therese Marie Oeming
Ethel O'Neill
Nan Pace
Nancy Princing
Sue Pumford
Sally Purcell
Cynthia Putnam
Patricia Raymond

Virginia Remensnyder
Francine Rifkin
Marcia Rilko
Mary Rockwell
Cathy Rousseau
Jeanne Schirmer
Karyl Scorsone
Patricia Shaheen
Patricia Shek
Amelia Smith
Janis Smith
Kathie Smith
Margaret Snelling
Susan Sonntag
Beverlee Spence
Julie Ann Stevens
Janet Stringer
Josephine Strobel
Leticia Stroebel
Carol Symons
Bernice Szczypka
Joan Talbot
Katharine Tessin
Carol Troester
Kathlyn Tuckey
Nancy Umbach
Mary Ellen Vaydik
Betty Webb
Judy Weldy
Catherine Wendland
Joan Wendland
Helene Whitehead
Rebecca Williams
Jane Ann Wright

Between the Lakes

Lake Superior Sponsors

APPETIZER CHAPTER SPONSOR
Horizons Conference Center

MAIN COURSE CHAPTER SPONSOR
Dow Chemical Company Foundation

SIDE DISH CHAPTER SPONSOR
West Saginaw County Chapter of Thrivent
Financial for Lutherans

DESSERT CHAPTER SPONSOR
Michigan Sugar Company

Lake Michigan Sponsors

JUNIOR LEAGUE OF SAGINAW VALLEY ACTIVES

Erin Gaynor
Cathy and Jim Jesko
Renee Johnston

Deb Kettling
Jackie Light
Karen and Jeff Newman
Dawn and Matt Pumford

Janeen Sheridan
Ursula Steckert
Tara and Mark Stewart

Lake Huron Sponsors

In Memory of Joseph Thomas Mitrzyk
Michigan Apple Committee
Lester Webb, M.D.–PC
Saint Mary's Foundation
The Rehmann Group

Lake Ontario Sponsors

Deisler Funeral Home
Garber Management Group
MCVI (Michigan CardioVascular Institute)
SC Johnson & Son
The Diabetic Foot Center

Lake Erie Sponsors

Anonymous
Bavarian Inn Lodge
Bay Valley Hotel and Resort
Bierlein Companies

Bintz Ski and Snowboard Shop
Crumbs Gourmet Cookie Café
Pizza Sams
The Fordney Club

The Rifkin Group
Tony's Block Plaza
Tri-Star Trust Bank
W. L. Case & Company

Saginaw Bay Sponsors

Katie Flegenheimer   Riverside Family Restaurant

In-Kind Donors

Ampro
Greg Hazen
Ruth Howell

Marshall Field's
Michigan Cherry Commission
Michigan Department of Agriculture

Marti Lisik
Jeff Oppermann
The Bird's Nest

Between the Lakes Committee

CHAIRMAN
Susie Nielsen

NON-RECIPE TEXT
Anne Flegenheimer

PHOTOGRAPHY AND COVER DESIGN
Marti Lisik
Janeen Sheridan
Susan Sonntag
Nancy Umbach

RECIPE COLLECTION
Cyndy Lange

SPONSORSHIP
Erin Gaynor

TREASURER
Elizabeth Stansbury

COMMITTEE MEMBERS

Sandy Donahue	Marcia Hoffman	Cathy Rousseau
Jennie Doyle	Julie Hohwart	Sarah Shemanski
Linda Fettig	Josephine Lee	Ursula Steckert
Paulette Genco	Karen McNish	Betty Webb
Catherin Hall	Betsy Meyer	Joan Wendland
Louise Harrison	Nan Pace	Jane Ann Wright
	Sally Purcell	

Between the Lakes

Recipe Contributors

Mary Ahrens
Laura Allen
Alice Baldwin
Elissa Basil
Leann Bauer
Kay Baumgarten
Bavarian Inn Lodge
Anne Beckley
Elizabeth Benjamin
Joan Bintz
Dorothy Borchard
Carolyn Bovill
Bonnie Braun
Ruth Braun
Kim Burau
Chris Burns
Octavia Cabey
Ruth Cherry
Katherine Church
Elizabeth Cilfone
Margaret Clark
Joanne Cline
Elizabeth Cornwell
Abby Day
Annette Deibel
Patrice Deisler
Karen Demetriou
Lisa Depillos
Corrine Dill
Saundra Donahue
Alma Doud
Jennie Doyle
Dixie Drinan
Dawn Eastman
Barb Ewend
Judith Farley
Katie Fifer
Anne Flegenheimer

Marge Flegenheimer
Veronica Furlo
Sandra Galsterer
Anne Gardner
Erin Gaynor
Mary Goedert
Sally Goin
Robin Greene
Jack Gustin
Catherin Hall
Vera Hanisko
Louise Harrison
Constance Harvey
Meg Hayes
Chris Hazen
Heatherfield's Restaurant
Mary Jo Heitman
Hillary Henderson
Mary Hill
Julie Hohwart
Melanie Hollman
Martha Humphreys
LeAnne Iamurri
Cathy Jesko
Renee Johnston
Sarah Jury
Peggy Kandulski
Elizabeth Kelly
Gerry Kelly
Sheryl Kendrick
Carrie Kessel
Joyce Kessel
Caroline Knowlton
Nancy Kraus
Barbara Krohn
Joyce Lamb
Cyndy Lange
Patricia Learman

Josephine Lee
Katheryn Lewis
Barbara Lincoln
Sandra Lusars
Nancy MacRae
Ginny Mahar
Joan Martin
Jessica McCallum
Judy McGovern
Joanne McLeod
Betsy Meyer
Michigan Apple Committee
Katharyn Morley
Sue Morley
Andrea Muladore
Sara Harvey Newell
Karen Newman
Mary Nicola
Susie Nielsen
Georgia Northway
Julie Nunn
Therese Marie Oeming
Dort O'Laughlin
Ethel O'Neill
Nan Pace
Deanna Patton
Maija Preston
Lynne Provenzano
Dawn Pumford
Sue Pumford
Sally Purcell
Patricia Raymond
Lori Reetz
Jean Richardson
Francine Rifkin
Rae Ann Roche
Catherine Rousseau
Barbara Russell

Jeanne Schirmer
Nancy Seamon
Lisa Seelye
Patricia Shek
Janeen Sheridan
Arloa Shreve
Molly Smith
Margaret Snelling
Susan Sonntag
Beverlee Spence
Marcia Spence
Nancy Spence
Marilyn Spencer
Elizabeth Stansbury
Ursula Steckert
Sue Stemler
Suzanne Stenglein
Colleen Stertz
Julie Stevens
Bonnie Stewart
Josephine Strobel
Judy Stuart
Elizabeth Stuber
Sue Sulfridge
Carol Symons
Bernice Szczypka
Lucy Thomson
Nancy Umbach
Mary Ellen Vaydik
Kate Weadock
Betty Webb
Judy Weldy
Joan Wendland
Amy Wierda
Peggy Wiltse
Bebe Wolgast
Jane Ann Wright

Artist Biographies

RUTH HOWELL

Ruth Spielman Howell is a local artist recognized for her ability to capture intrigue in the ordinary. Raised in Dearborn, Michigan, Ruth's interest in art was encouraged by her parents from an early age. Ruth holds a Bachelor of Fine Arts from the University of Michigan, School of Architecture and Design. Her formal studies continued at the Center for Creative Studies in Detroit, Michigan. For eight years she was employed as an artist doing product illustration and layout work. After a hiatus for marriage and children, she returned to the art world, pursuing a career in drawing, painting, and teaching art. Currently Ruth shares her knowledge and talent at the Midland Center for the Arts, the Saginaw Art Museum, and local schools. Her exhibition record includes the Great Lakes Regional Art Exhibition and the Annual State of the Arts Exhibition, Special Merit Award.

MARTI LISIK

Martha Lisik is a portrait photographer and graphic artist for the family business, Portraits by Gregg and Associates. Working with her parents has afforded her the opportunity to combine traditional portrait skills with artistic applications and graphic design. She has been recognized by both Kodak and Fuji for her outstanding wedding and portrait photography. Martha and her husband, Bryce, are residents of Saginaw County, where Martha is an active member of the Junior League of Saginaw Valley.

GREG HAZEN

Greg Hazen started taking photography classes with his father at the age of fifteen. Many of his photos have been taken underwater while diving, and others reflect his love of nature and wildlife. He also takes great pride in the photos of his wife and three children. He has given many of his photos to nonprofit organizations for auction. Greg is an ophthalmologist in the Saginaw area and specializes in ocular-plastics.

Contents

Mission Statement

The Junior League of Saginaw Valley is an organization of women committed to promoting voluntarism, developing the potential of women, and improving the community through the effective action and leadership of trained volunteers. Its purpose is exclusively educational and charitable.

The Junior League of Saginaw Valley reaches out to women regardless of race, creed, religion, or national origin who demonstrate an interest in and a commitment to voluntarism.

History

The Junior League of Saginaw Valley has dedicated volunteer funds and time to the following community agencies:

Bay County Women's Center
Cathedral District Youth Center
Child Abuse and Neglect Council
Child & Family Services of Midland
City Rescue Mission
Court Appointed Special Advocate of Saginaw County
First Ward Community Center
Frankenmuth Historical Museum
Hartley Outdoor Nature Center
Hospital Hospitality House
Marshall Fredericks Sculpture Gallery
Midland Shelterhouse
Midland's Children's Museum
Saginaw Art Museum
Saginaw Children's Zoo and Carousel
Saginaw Community Enrichment Commission
Saginaw Community Foundation
Saginaw Symphony Young People's Concert Association
Success By Six
Temple Theatre Arts Association
Underground Railroad
United for Kids Children's Assessment Center
Voluntary Action Center

Between the Lakes

Appetizers and Beverages

Antipasto Bowl
Shrimp with Red Onions and Capers
Mushrooms in Marinade
Merry Tomatoes
Bacon Roll-Ups
Pepperoni Bites
Taco Tartlets
Chicken and Bacon Nuggets
Crab Rangoon
Mediterranean Spinach Bites
Angel Hair Flans
Sinful Spuds
Blue Cheese Popovers
Hot Ryes
Savory Party Bread
Grilled Brie with Tomatoes
Kielbasa with Mustard Cream
Chicken Liver Mousse
Layered Oriental Spread
Seafood Snack
Shrimp Curry Spread
Layered Bacon Appetizer
Cheese Almond Spread
Maui Cheese Dip
Mozzarella Dip
Vidalia Onion Dip
Black Bean and Corn Salsa
Jezebel Sauce
Curried Candied Pecans
Sweet and Spicy Nuts
Company Punch
Pink Punch

Appetizers and Beverages

Antipasto Bowl

1 1/2 pounds skinless smoked sausage,
      thinly sliced
1   pound peeled cooked shrimp
2   (14-ounce) cans artichoke hearts,
      drained and quartered
2   (6-ounce) jars whole mushrooms,
      drained
1   (4-ounce) can black olives, pitted
      and drained
12   ounces cubed mozzarella cheese
1   (14-ounce) can hearts of palm,
      cut into bite-size pieces
2   garlic cloves
1/2   cup vegetable oil
1/4   cup white wine vinegar
1/4   cup fresh basil
1/4   cup fresh parsley
1/2   teaspoon salt
1/4   teaspoon pepper

Combine the sausage, shrimp, artichoke
hearts, mushrooms, olives, cheese and
hearts of palm in a large shallow bowl.
   Combine the garlic, oil, vinegar, basil,
parsley, salt and pepper in a food processor
and process until the herbs are minced.
   Pour over the sausage mixture and
mix well. Marinate, covered, in the
refrigerator for several hours. Serve cold
with wooden picks.

   Variation: Add baby corn and grape
tomatoes and toss with the sausage mixture.

Serves 30

Shrimp with Red Onions and Capers

2   pounds medium peeled cooked shrimp
2   cups sliced red onions
7   or 8 bay leaves
2 1/2 tablespoons capers with liquid
      Dash of Tabasco sauce
1 1/2 cups vegetable oil
3/4   cup vinegar
1 1/2 teaspoons celery seeds

Layer the shrimp and onion slices in
a large bowl. Combine the bay leaves,
capers, Tabasco sauce, oil, vinegar and
celery seeds in a bowl and stir. Pour the
dressing over the shrimp. Marinate,
covered, in the refrigerator for 24 hours.
Discard the bay leaves before serving.
Serve with party rye bread.

Serves 20

Mushrooms in Marinade

Bavarian Inn Lodge

2   pounds mushrooms
3¹/4 cups vegetable oil
1¹/4 cups distilled vinegar
1   cup tarragon vinegar
1¹/2 tablespoons salt
1¹/2 teaspoons dry mustard
1¹/2 teaspoons sugar
2¹/2 teaspoons pepper
3/4   cup minced onion
1¹/2 teaspoons chopped garlic

Clean the mushrooms well and set aside in a large bowl. Combine the oil, distilled vinegar and tarragon vinegar in a bowl and mix well. Slowly add the salt, mustard, sugar and pepper, stirring constantly to prevent lumps. Stir in the onion and garlic. Pour the marinade over the mushrooms. Marinate, covered, in the refrigerator for 2 to 4 days.

Serves about 20

Merry Tomatoes

30   to 40 cherry tomatoes,
     stems removed
1   cup vodka
1   tablespoon celery salt
3/4 teaspoon lemon pepper

Toss the tomatoes with the vodka in a bowl. Marinate, covered, in the refrigerator for 8 to 12 hours. Stir the celery salt and lemon pepper together in a small bowl. To serve, spear a tomato with a wooden pick and dip in the celery salt mixture.

Serves 30 to 40

Between the Lakes

Bacon Roll-Ups

6   thin slices white sandwich bread
1   jar Old English cheese spread
12   slices bacon

Trim the bread crusts. Lightly flatten the bread slices with a rolling pin. Gently spread about 1 tablespoon cheese spread on each bread slice and roll up tightly. Cut each into halves. Wrap a slice of bacon around each half and secure with a wooden pick. Place on a nonstick baking sheet. Bake at 375 degrees for 10 minutes or until the bacon is crisp and the bread is browned.

Serves 12

Pepperoni Bites

1   cup finely chopped pepperoni
1   cup (4 ounces) shredded Swiss cheese
1   tomato, finely chopped
1   small onion, chopped
3/4 cup mayonnaise
1   teaspoon basil
2   (10-ounce) packages refrigerator flaky biscuits

Combine the pepperoni, cheese, tomato, onion, mayonnaise and basil in a bowl and mix together. Cut each biscuit into halves horizontally. Place the biscuit halves in greased miniature muffin cups, pressing to fit. Spoon 1 tablespoon pepperoni mixture into each cup. Bake at 350 degrees for 20 to 25 minutes or until golden brown. Serve warm.

Note: These freeze very well.

Serves 40

ONIONS
Hold onions under water or refrigerate prior to peeling or cutting to neutralize the atoms that cause watery eyes. Rubbing hands with lemon will remove the onion smell. Onions will keep if they are stored where air can circulate around them—hanging them in a string bag is an excellent storage technique. Onions are rich in vitamins C and B6, and potassium.

Taco Tartlets

1   pound ground beef
1   envelope taco seasoning mix
2   tablespoons ice cold water
1   cup sour cream
1/4   cup taco sauce
1   (2-ounce) can sliced pitted black olives, drained
3/4   cup crushed taco chips
1/2   cup (2 ounces) shredded taco cheese or sharp Cheddar cheese

Combine the ground beef, taco seasoning mix and water in a bowl. Press the ground beef mixture into 12 miniature muffin cups, forming a shell.

Stir the sour cream, taco sauce, black olives and crushed taco chips together in a bowl. Spoon the sour cream mixture into the ground beef shells. Sprinkle the cheese over each tartlet. Bake at 375 degrees for 10 minutes. Remove the tartlets and drain on paper towels.

Note: Taco tartlets may be baked and frozen. Reheat the frozen tartlets at 350 degrees for 20 minutes.

Serves 12

Chicken and Bacon Nuggets

3   large boneless skinless chicken breasts
1/4   cup reduced-sugar apricot preserves
2   tablespoons reduced-sodium soy sauce
1/2   teaspoon each salt and ginger
1/8   teaspoon garlic powder
1   pound sliced bacon

Cut the chicken breasts lengthwise into thirds. Cut each strip into 1 1/2-inch squares.

Combine the chicken and the next 5 ingredients in a bowl. Marinate, covered, in the refrigerator for 3 to 4 hours.

Arrange the bacon slices on a rack in a broiler pan. Bake at 350 degrees for 10 to 12 minutes. Remove the bacon to paper towels to drain. Cut the bacon crosswise into halves. Remove the chicken from the marinade, reserving the marinade. Pour the reserved marinade into a small saucepan. Boil for 2 to 3 minutes, stirring constantly.

Wrap a bacon slice around each piece of chicken and secure with a wooden pick. Place the chicken on a rack in a broiler pan. Bake for 8 minutes. Turn the chicken and brush with the reserved marinade. Bake for 8 minutes longer or until the bacon is crisp and the chicken is cooked through.

Note: This would also be good with chicken livers or water chestnuts to replace the chicken.

Serves 12

Between the Lakes

Crab Rangoon

2   (3-ounce) packages cream cheese,
    softened
8   ounces fresh or frozen crab meat,
    thawed
1   green onion, chopped
1   tablespoon minced fresh gingerroot
1   egg white
1/2 (16-ounce) package won ton
    wrappers
    Vegetable oil for deep frying

Combine the cream cheese, crab meat,
green onion and gingerroot in a bowl. Brush
the egg white on the corners of each won
ton wrapper. Place about 1 teaspoon crab
mixture in the center of each wrapper. Pull
the corners in to form a point and press to
seal. Fry the won ton in hot oil in a skillet
for 3 to 4 minutes or until lightly browned.

Serves about 25

Mediterranean Spinach Bites

1   (11-ounce) package refrigerated fresh
    bread dough
1   (10-ounce) package frozen chopped
    spinach, thawed and drained
1   plum tomato, seeded and chopped
1/4 cup chopped onion
1   garlic clove, pressed
1/2 cup (2 ounces) crumbled feta cheese
1/4 cup mayonnaise
1/4 cup sour cream
1/2 teaspoon dill weed
1/4 teaspoon salt

Prepare the bread according to package
directions. Cool and slice 1/4 inch thick.
Combine the spinach, tomato, onion, garlic,
cheese, mayonnaise, sour cream, dill weed
and salt in a medium bowl and mix well.
Spoon the spinach mixture on bread slices
and spread to cover. Place on a baking
sheet. Bake at 375 degrees for 10 to
12 minutes. Serve hot.

Serves 12

Angel Hair Flans

3   ounces angel hair pasta
3   eggs
1   cup heavy cream
1/2   teaspoon nutmeg
1   teaspoon salt
    Freshly ground pepper to taste
1   cup (4 ounces) grated Parmesan
    cheese

Bring a large pan of water to a boil. Add the angel hair pasta and cook according to package directions; drain. Divide the pasta evenly among 24 miniature muffin cups or 12 regular-size muffin cups sprayed with nonstick cooking spray. Set aside. Combine the eggs, cream, nutmeg, salt, pepper and 2/3 cup of the cheese in a bowl and mix well. Spoon the mixture into the prepared cups. Sprinkle on the remaining 1/3 cup cheese.

Bake at 350 degrees for 15 to 20 minutes for miniature muffin cups and 25 to 30 minutes for regular-size muffin cups or until the flans are set and lightly browned. Remove from the oven and cool 10 minutes. Gently lift the flans from the cups.

Note: The flans can be baked up to 3 days in advance. Let stand until cool. Chill, covered, for up to 3 days. Reheat at 350 degrees for 10 to 15 minutes.

Serves 12

Sinful Spuds

12   small new potatoes, uniform size
1 1/2   teaspoons kosher salt
1/2   cup (2 ounces) feta cheese
1/4   cup toasted pine nuts
2   tablespoons chopped green olives
1   tablespoon extra-virgin olive oil
1   tablespoon dried currants
1/2   teaspoon chopped lemon zest
1/4   teaspoon oregano
1/4   teaspoon pepper
24   parsley leaves

Cut a thin slice off the top and bottom of each potato. Cut the potatoes crosswise into halves. Combine the potatoes with salt and enough water to cover in a saucepan. Boil until tender; drain. Let stand until cool. Crumble the cheese into a small bowl. Add the pine nuts, olives, olive oil, currants, lemon zest, oregano and pepper and mix well.

Scoop out the potato centers with a spoon or melon baller. Add a spoonful of the cheese mixture to each potato. Garnish with a parsley leaf.

Note: Make the cheese mixture without the pine nuts and chill, covered, for up to 2 days. Bring the mixture to room temperature and stir in the pine nuts just before serving.

Serves 24

Between the Lakes

Blue Cheese Popovers

2	eggs
1	cup milk, at room temperature
2	tablespoons unsalted butter, melted
1	cup flour
1/2	teaspoon kosher salt
1/8	teaspoon pepper
5	tablespoons crumbled blue cheese
1	tablespoon chopped fresh thyme

Combine the eggs, milk, melted butter, flour, salt and pepper in a large bowl and mix well until the lumps are dissolved. Whisk in the cheese and thyme. Pour into a container with an airtight lid. Chill for 2 to 12 hours. Generously butter 24 miniature muffin cups. Fill each cup to the top with the chilled batter. Bake at 425 degrees on top oven rack for 18 to 20 minutes or until the popovers are golden brown and puffed.

Makes 24 popovers

Hot Ryes

1	cup (4 ounces) shredded Swiss cheese
1/4	cup crumbled crisp-cooked bacon
1/2	cup finely chopped onion
1	teaspoon Worcestershire sauce
1/4	teaspoon salt
1/4	cup mayonnaise
1	loaf cocktail rye bread or rye crackers

Combine the cheese, bacon, onion, Worcestershire sauce, salt and mayonnaise in a bowl. Spread the cheese mixture on the bread and arrange on a greased baking sheet. Bake at 300 degrees for 15 minutes.

Serves 20

FLOWERS

Many people are surprised to learn that Michigan is the nation's leading producer of geraniums, hanging flower baskets, and Easter lilies and the second leading producer of gladiolus and flats of bedding plants. Holland, Michigan has hosted the Tulip Time Festival for the past 75 years. The spectacular Lilac Festival is held on Mackinac Island each June.

Savory Party Bread

1   round loaf sourdough bread
16 ounces Monterey Jack cheese, sliced
1/2 cup (1 stick) butter
1/2 cup chopped green onions
1   tablespoon poppy seeds

Make lengthwise and crosswise cuts in the bread, but do not slice through the bread. Place some of the cheese in each cut. Place the bread on a large sheet of foil on a baking sheet. Melt the butter in a small saucepan. Add the onions and poppy seeds. Pour the butter mixture over the bread. Fold the foil over the bread. Bake at 350 degrees for 15 minutes. Uncover the top of the bread and bake for 10 to 15 minutes longer or until the bread is browned.

Serves 8 to 12

Grilled Brie with Tomatoes

3   plum tomatoes, seeded and diced
1   garlic clove, finely chopped
4   or 5 fresh basil leaves, torn into
    small pieces
2   tablespoons olive oil
    Salt and pepper to taste
1   (14-ounce) wheel Brie cheese

Combine the tomatoes, garlic, basil, olive oil, salt and pepper in a medium bowl. Let stand for 15 minutes for flavors to blend. Cut the cheese horizontally into halves. Place one half cut side up on a sheet of heavy-duty foil large enough to completely wrap the cheese. Spread the tomato mixture on the cheese. Top with the remaining cheese cut side down. Wrap completely in foil and place on a grill rack. Grill over medium-hot coals for 15 to 20 minutes. Remove from the grill. Arrange on a serving plate with crusty bread.

Serves about 14

Between the Lakes

Kielbasa with Mustard Cream

2   pounds kielbasa or smoked sausage,
     cut into bite-size pieces
1   (12-ounce) can beer
1/4 cup brandy
1/2 cup sour cream
1/2 cup mayonnaise
1   tablespoon dry mustard
1/2 teaspoon vinegar
1   tablespoon chopped green onions

Combine the kielbasa and beer in a baking dish. Bake at 325 degrees for 1 hour. Add the brandy and bake for 15 minutes longer. Spoon the kielbasa into a chafing dish or fondue pot. Combine the sour cream, mayonnaise, mustard, vinegar and green onions in a bowl and mix well. Serve the kielbasa with mustard cream for dipping.

Serves 32

Chicken Liver Mousse

1   pound chicken livers
2   tablespoons butter
2   tablespoons minced shallot or
     green onions
1/3 cup madeira or Cognac
1/4 cup heavy cream
1/2 teaspoon salt
1/8 teaspoon allspice
1/8 teaspoon pepper
     Pinch of thyme
1/2 cup (1 stick) butter, melted

Cut the livers into 1/2-inch pieces. Melt 2 tablespoons butter in a large skillet. Add the livers and shallot and sauté for 2 or 3 minutes or until the livers are firm, but pink inside. Remove livers and shallot to a blender. Pour the madeira into the skillet and cook over high heat until the liquid is reduced to 3 tablespoons. Add the madeira to the blender. Add the cream, salt, allspice, pepper and thyme. Cover and process to form a smooth paste. Add 1/2 cup melted butter and blend for several seconds. Remove the liver mixture from the blender and force through a fine sieve with a wooden spoon. Place the liver mousse in a serving bowl. Adjust the seasonings. Chill, covered, for 2 to 3 hours.

Serves 10

Layered Oriental Spread

3/4   cup chopped cooked chicken
1/2   cup shredded carrots
1/2   cup chopped peanuts, cashews or water chestnuts, or a combination of each
3   tablespoons sliced green onions
1   tablespoon chopped fresh parsley
1   garlic clove, minced
2   tablespoons soy sauce
1/4   teaspoon ginger
     Dash of sesame oil (optional)
1   (8-ounce) package cream cheese, softened
1   tablespoon milk
1   cup (about) sweet and sour sauce

Combine the chicken, carrots, peanuts, green onions, parsley, garlic, soy sauce and ginger in a medium bowl. Add a dash of sesame oil and mix well. Chill, covered, for 4 to 12 hours.

Combine the cream cheese and milk in a bowl and mix well. Spread the cream cheese on a round plate. Top with the chicken mixture. Drizzle with sweet and sour sauce. Serve with crackers.

Serves 10 to 12

Seafood Snack

1 1/2   cups (6 ounces) shredded Cheddar cheese
1   (4-ounce) can diced green chiles, drained
1   (2-ounce) can sliced pitted black olives, drained
1/3   cup sliced green onions
1/4   cup mayonnaise
1   (4-ounce) can baby shrimp, drained and rinsed
36   to 40 round tortilla chips

Combine the cheese, chiles, olives, green onions and mayonnaise in a large bowl. Gently fold in the shrimp. Place the shrimp mixture in an ovenproof dish. Bake at 350 degrees for 20 minutes. Serve with the tortilla chips.

Note: To cook in a microwave oven, arrange 20 tortilla chips on a microwave-safe platter. Top each chip with a rounded teaspoon of the cheese mixture. Microwave, uncovered, on High for 1 to 2 minutes or until the cheese melts, turning the plate a half-turn after 1 minute. Repeat with the remaining chips and shrimp mixture.

Serves 36 to 40

Shrimp Curry Spread

1   (8-ounce) package cream cheese,
      softened
1   tablespoon curry powder
1/4 teaspoon garlic powder
1/4 cup Major Grey mango chutney,
      cut into small pieces
1   cup cooked shrimp, cut into small
      pieces
1   cup chopped nuts
1/2 cup sour cream
2   tablespoons milk

Combine the cream cheese, curry
powder, garlic powder and chutney in a
bowl and mix well. Stir in the shrimp, nuts,
sour cream and milk. If the mixture is too
stiff to spread, add a little more milk. Spoon
the mixture into a small bowl. Serve with
toast, crackers or vegetables.

Serves 40

Layered Bacon Appetizer

1   (8-ounce) package cream cheese or
       light cream cheese, softened
1/2   cup (2 ounces) shredded
       Cheddar cheese
1/2   teaspoon curry powder
       Few drops of Tabasco sauce
1   (10-ounce) jar chutney
2 1/2 cups (10 ounces) shredded
       Cheddar cheese
6   slices of bacon, crisp-cooked and
       crumbled
6   green onions, chopped

Combine the cream cheese, 1/2 cup
Cheddar cheese, curry powder and a few
drops of Tabasco sauce in a medium bowl
and mix well. Spread the mixture evenly
over an 8- to 10-inch serving dish. Spread
the chutney over the cheese layer. Top with
the remaining 2 1/2 cups Cheddar cheese,
bacon and green onions. Serve with
crackers and celery sticks.

Serves 10 to 12

Cheese Almond Spread

10 ounces Cracker Barrel medium Cheddar cheese, shredded
8   ounces bacon, crisp-cooked, crumbled
4   green onions, finely chopped
3   tablespoons sliced almonds, toasted
3/4 cup mayonnaise

Combine the cheese and bacon in a large bowl. Add the green onions, almonds and mayonnaise and mix well. Chill, covered, for up to 24 hours. Serve with crackers.

Serves 20

Maui Cheese Dip

1   (6-ounce) jar pineapple preserves
4   to 6 tablespoons Dijon mustard, or to taste
1   (12-ounce) container soft
    cream cheese
1/2 cup slivered almonds, toasted

Combine the preserves, mustard, cream cheese and almonds in a bowl and mix well. Chill, covered, for several hours. Serve the dip with crackers or fresh fruit.

Serves 12

GRAPES
Michigan has 13,500 acres of vineyards making it the fourth largest grape-growing state. About 1,500 acres are devoted to wine grapes, making the state eighth in wine grape production. Michigan's 39 wineries produce more than 200,000 cases of wine annually, ranking 13th in wine production in the country.

Between the Lakes

Mozzarella Dip

4   cups (16 ounces) shredded
     mozzarella cheese
1   cup mayonnaise
1/3 cup chopped onion
1   (4-ounce) can chopped green chiles
1   tablespoon chopped jalapeño chile
     Dash of Worcestershire sauce
     Dash of garlic powder

Combine the cheese, mayonnaise, onion, green chiles, jalapeño chile, Worcestershire sauce and garlic powder in a large bowl and mix well. Spoon into a baking dish. Bake at 350 degrees for 30 minutes.

Serves 50

Vidalia Onion Dip

Since Vidalia onions are only available during the spring and early summer you may have to substitute another sweet onion variety in this recipe.

1   cup chopped Vidalia onion
1   cup mayonnaise
1   cup (4 ounces) shredded Swiss, Emmentaler or Gruyère cheese

Combine the onion, mayonnaise and cheese in a medium bowl and mix well. Spoon into a buttered 1 1/2-quart baking dish. Bake at 350 degrees for 20 minutes or until the mixture is bubbly. Serve with toast triangles or crackers.

Note: This can also be served in a fondue pot.

Serves 20

Black Bean and Corn Salsa

1	(15-ounce) can black beans, drained	1/3	cup chopped fresh cilantro
1	(15-ounce) can corn, drained	1/3	cup lime juice
1	bunch scallions, diced	1	tablespoon olive oil
1	Roma tomato, diced	1	teaspoon cumin
1/2	red bell pepper, diced	1	avocado, cut into bite-size chunks

Combine the black beans, corn, scallions, tomato, bell pepper, cilantro, lime juice, olive oil and cumin in a large bowl and mix well. Stir in the avocado. Chill, covered, for several hours. Serve with chips.

Serves 40

Jezebel Sauce

1	(8-ounce) jar pineapple preserves	1	tablespoon ground pepper
1	(8-ounce) jar apple jelly	1	(5-ounce) jar white horseradish
2	tablespoons dry mustard		

Combine the pineapple preserves, apple jelly, dry mustard, pepper and horseradish in a bowl and stir to mix well. Chill, covered, at least 1 day before serving.

To serve, spread the sauce over cream cheese and accompany with crackers.

Note: Refrigerate leftovers up to 1 month in a tightly-covered container.

Makes about 3 cups

Curried Candied Pecans

1 1/2 teaspoons onion powder
1 1/2 teaspoons garlic powder
1   teaspoon kosher salt
3/4   teaspoon curry powder
1/4   teaspoon cayenne pepper
2   tablespoons unsalted butter
2   tablespoons honey
1/4   teaspoon kosher salt
3   cups pecan halves
      Sugar for coating (optional)

Combine the onion powder, garlic powder, 1 teaspoon kosher salt, curry powder and cayenne pepper in a small bowl and stir to mix well.

Melt the butter, honey and 1/4 teaspoon kosher salt in a heavy medium saucepan over medium heat. Add the pecans and stir to coat. Remove from the heat. Add the seasoning mixture and toss to coat the pecans evenly. Spread the pecans on a 10×15-inch baking pan lined with foil. Bake at 250 degrees for 40 minutes or until the pecans are dry and toasted. Cool completely and separate the pecans. Sprinkle with sugar.

Note: The pecans can be made a week in advance and stored in an airtight container at room temperature.

Makes 3 cups

Sweet and Spicy Nuts

6   tablespoons unsalted butter
1/2   cup packed brown sugar
1/4   cup water
1   tablespoon chili powder
1 1/2 teaspoons salt
1   teaspoon ground cumin
1   teaspoon oregano
1/2   teaspoon ground black pepper
1/4   teaspoon cayenne pepper
2   cups walnut halves
2   cups pecan halves
2   cups whole almonds

Melt the butter in a large nonstick skillet over medium heat. Add the brown sugar, water, chili powder, salt, cumin, oregano, black pepper and cayenne pepper. Stir for 1 minute or until the sugar dissolves. Add the walnuts, pecans and almonds. Stir 2 minutes or until the butter coats the nuts.

Spread the nuts in a single layer on a large baking sheet sprayed with nonstick cooking spray. Bake at 300 degrees for 25 minutes or until the nuts are glazed and deep brown, stirring often. Cool completely on the baking sheet, stirring occasionally.

Note: Store the nuts in an airtight container at room temperature.

Serves 24

Company Punch

2 1/2 cups Southern Comfort
3/4 cup lemon juice, chilled
2 (6-ounce) cans frozen lemonade concentrate, thawed
1 (6-ounce) can frozen orange juice concentrate, thawed
1 liter lemon-lime soda, chilled
   Orange and lemon slices

Combine the Southern Comfort, lemon juice, lemonade concentrate and orange juice concentrate in a large punch bowl. Pour in the lemon-lime soda just before serving. Float the orange and lemon slices on the punch.

Serves 20

Pink Punch

1/2 gallon raspberry sherbet
1 pound frozen sliced strawberries
1 (14-ounce) can pineapple juice, chilled
2 liters ginger ale, chilled

Scoop the sherbet into a large punch bowl. Add the strawberries and pineapple juice. Pour in the ginger ale just before serving.

Serves about 40

Between the Lakes

Breads and Breakfast

Saginaw Bay Cinnamon Rolls
Orange Sticky Buns
French Bread
Cherry Oatmeal Bread
Orange Nut Bread
Sour Cream Coffee Cake
Blueberry Muffins
Refrigerator Bran Muffins
Cherry Crumb Muffins
Raspberry Cheesecake Muffins
Apple French Toast
Crème Brûlée French Toast
Blueberry Pancakes
Sour Cream Pancakes
Sunday Breakfast
Apple Lasagna
Baked Oatmeal
Ham and Egg Bake
Baked Egg Roll
Junior League of Saginaw Breakfast Eggs
Elegant Eggs
Brunch Enchiladas
Sausage Ring
Morel Quiche
Wild Rice Quiche
Pita Sandwich
Hot Spiced Fruit Compote
No-Brainer Breakfast in a Glass

Breads and Breakfast

Saginaw Bay Cinnamon Rolls

1/2 cup milk
2 tablespoons sugar
2 tablespoons butter
1/4 teaspoon salt
1 small egg, lightly beaten
1 envelope dry yeast
2 tablespoons lukewarm water
2 cups minus 2 tablespoons flour
2 tablespoons lard
4 teaspoons butter
1/2 cup plus 2 tablespoons packed brown sugar
    Cinnamon for sprinkling
2/3 cup sifted confectioners' sugar
    Milk

Bring 1/2 cup milk to a boil in a saucepan. Add the sugar, 2 tablespoons butter and salt. Add the egg and set aside to cool. Dissolve the yeast in the warm water in a cup. Add the yeast to the egg mixture. Stir in the flour a little at a time to form soft dough. Remove the dough to a well-greased bowl, turning to coat the surface. Cover with waxed paper and let rise in a warm place for 1 hour or until doubled in bulk. Melt the lard and 4 teaspoons butter in a small saucepan; set aside. Roll the dough into an oblong shape 1/3 inch thick. Spread with the lard mixture. Sprinkle with the brown sugar. Generously sprinkle with cinnamon. Roll as for a jelly roll, sealing the edge. Cut into slices 1 inch thick. Place the slices cut side up in a greased 9×11-inch baking pan. Let rise for 30 minutes. Bake at 350 degrees for 20 to 25 minutes or until light brown. Combine the confectioners' sugar with enough milk for spreading in a small bowl. Spread the confectioners' sugar glaze over the cinnamon buns while still warm.

Makes about 1 dozen rolls

Orange Sticky Buns

1/4   cup (1/2 stick) margarine or butter
1/4   cup packed brown sugar
1/2   cup flaked coconut
1/4   cup sliced or slivered almonds
1/2   cup orange marmalade
1/4   to 1/2 teaspoon grated gingerroot
1   (10-ounce) can refrigerated flaky biscuits

Combine the margarine, brown sugar, coconut and almonds in a mixing bowl. Spoon into a 5x9-inch loaf pan. Bake at 375 degrees until the margarine melts. Remove from the oven. Spread the coconut mixture evenly on the bottom of the pan. Combine the marmalade and gingerroot in a small bowl and set aside. Separate the dough into 10 biscuits. Spread about 2 teaspoons marmalade mixture on 1 side of each biscuit. Stand the biscuits on edge slightly overlapping in 2 rows of 5 biscuits each in the pan. Bake at 375 degrees for 25 to 30 minutes or until deep golden brown, covering the pan with foil during the last 15 minutes of baking to prevent overbaking. Cool for 4 minutes. Run a knife around the edges to loosen. Invert onto a serving plate.

Serves 10

French Bread

2   envelopes dry yeast
2 1/2   cups warm water
1   tablespoon salt
1   tablespoon butter, melted
7   cups flour
1/4   cup cornmeal
1   egg white
1   tablespoon cold water

Dissolve the yeast in the warm water in a large mixing bowl. Add the salt, butter and flour. Attach a dough hook to the mixer and mix on low speed for 2 minutes or until blended. Beat for 2 minutes longer. The dough will be sticky. Place the dough in a greased bowl, turning to coat the surface. Let rise, covered, in a warm place for 1 hour or until doubled in bulk. Punch the dough down and divide into 2 equal portions. Roll each into an 11×15-inch rectangle. Beginning on the long side, roll up tightly as for a jelly roll, sealing the edges. Taper the ends if desired.

Arrange each loaf on a greased baking sheet dusted with the cornmeal. Cover and let rise in a warm place for 1 hour or until doubled in bulk. Make 4 diagonal slashes on top of each loaf. Bake at 450 degrees for 25 minutes. Remove from the oven. Mix the egg white and cold water together in a bowl and brush on the loaves. Bake the loaves for 5 minutes longer. Remove the bread from the baking sheet and cool on a wire rack.

Note: For a crisp crust, fill a shallow pan 1/3 full with hot water. Place on the bottom of the oven. Halfway through baking, remove the water pan if the water hasn't evaporated. Do not glaze the loaves with egg white.

Makes 2 loaves

Cherry Oatmeal Bread

2   cups sifted flour
1   tablespoon baking powder
1/2   teaspoon baking soda
1/2   teaspoon salt
3/4   cup sugar
1   cup rolled oats
2   eggs
1/4   cup vegetable oil
1   cup milk
1   cup dried cherries

Sift the flour, baking powder, baking soda, salt and sugar into a large bowl. Stir in the rolled oats. Beat the eggs in a bowl. Add the oil and milk and mix well. Stir into the flour mixture and mix well. Add the dried cherries. Pour into a greased 5×9-inch loaf pan. Bake at 350 degrees for 1 hour. Cool in the pan for 10 minutes. Remove to a wire rack and cool completely.

Serves about 10

Orange Nut Bread

2   cups sifted flour
1   teaspoon baking soda
3/4   teaspoon salt
1/2   cup sugar
1   egg, well beaten
3/4   cup strained orange juice
2   tablespoons lemon juice
1   teaspoon lemon zest
1   teaspoon orange zest
1/4   cup shortening
3/4   cup coarsely chopped pecans

Sift the flour into a bowl with the baking soda, salt and sugar. Combine the egg, orange juice, lemon juice, lemon zest, orange zest and shortening in a mixing bowl. Add to the dry ingredients and stir just until mixed. Stir in the pecans. Spoon the batter into a greased 5×9-inch loaf pan. Cover and let stand for 20 minutes. Bake at 350 degrees for 1 hour. Cool in the pan for 10 minutes. Remove to a wire rack and cool completely.

Serves 10

Sour Cream Coffee Cake

1   cup (2 sticks) butter, softened
2   cups sugar
2   eggs
1   cup sour cream
1   teaspoon vanilla extract
2   cups flour
1   teaspoon baking powder
1/2 teaspoon salt
4   or 5 teaspoons sugar
1   teaspoon cinnamon

Cream the butter and 2 cups sugar in a mixing bowl until light and creamy. Add the eggs 1 at a time, beating well after each addition. Blend the sour cream and vanilla in a bowl. Mix the flour, baking powder and salt in a bowl. Add the sour cream and flour mixture alternately to the creamed mixture, beating constantly. Mix 4 or 5 teaspoons sugar and cinnamon together. Spoon half the batter in a well-greased and floured bundt pan. Sprinkle with the cinnamon sugar. Top with the remaining batter. Bake at 350 degrees for 1 hour. Remove from the oven. Cool in the pan for 10 minutes. Invert onto a wire rack to cool completely.

Serves 16

Blueberry Muffins

1 1/2 cups flour
1/2 cup sugar
2   teaspoons baking powder
1/2 teaspoon salt
1   egg or equivalent egg substitute
1/2 cup skim milk
1/4 cup vegetable oil
1   cup fresh or frozen blueberries

Mix the first 4 ingredients in a mixing bowl. Whisk the egg, milk and oil in a bowl. Add to the dry ingredients and stir just until mixed. Fold in the blueberries. Spoon the batter into greased or lined muffin cups. Bake at 400 degrees for 20 minutes.

Makes 1 dozen

Refrigerator Bran Muffins

1   cup each shortening and boiling water
3   cups sugar
4   eggs, beaten
4   cups buttermilk
2   cups Bran Buds or All Bran
5   cups flour
5   teaspoons baking soda

Mix the ingredients in a large bowl. Chill, covered, for about 1 hour. Spoon into nonstick muffin cups. Bake at 350 degrees for 20 minutes.

Makes 3 to 4 dozen

Cherry Crumb Muffins

2   cups flour
1   tablespoon baking powder
1/2 cup sugar
1/4 teaspoon salt
1 1/4 cups cherries, pitted and
     coarsely chopped
1   egg
1/4 cup vegetable oil
1   cup milk
1/4 cup (1/2 stick) butter
1/3 cup packed brown sugar
1/2 teaspoon cinnamon
1/2 cup flour

Sift 2 cups flour, baking powder, sugar and salt into a large bowl. Add the cherries. Beat the egg, oil and milk in a bowl. Add to the dry ingredients and stir just until mixed. Spoon the batter into nonstick muffin cups, filling 2/3 full. Melt the butter in a small saucepan. Stir in the brown sugar, cinnamon and 1/2 cup flour. Sprinkle the crumb mixture over the muffin batter. Bake at 375 degrees for 30 minutes.

Makes 1 dozen

Raspberry Cheesecake Muffins

1   (3-ounce) package cream cheese,
     softened
1   egg
1/4 cup sugar
1/2 teaspoon vanilla extract
1   cup milk
6   tablespoons butter
1   teaspoon vanilla extract
2   eggs
2   cups flour
2 1/2 teaspoons baking powder
1/2 teaspoon salt
3/4 cup sugar
1   cup fresh or thawed frozen raspberries

Beat the cream cheese, 1 egg, 1/4 cup sugar and 1/2 teaspoon vanilla in a small mixing bowl until smooth. Set aside. Combine the milk, butter and 1 teaspoon vanilla in a saucepan. Cook over medium heat until the butter melts, stirring constantly. Cool until warm to the touch. Beat in 2 eggs. Set aside. Combine the flour, baking powder, salt and 3/4 cup sugar in a mixing bowl. Add the milk mixture and stir just until mixed. Fold in the raspberries. Spoon the batter into nonstick muffin cups. Spoon about 2 teaspoons cream cheese mixture over the batter in each muffin cup. Pull a knife through the top to swirl slightly. Bake at 400 degrees for 20 minutes or until the muffins spring back when lightly touched. Remove from the oven.

Makes 1 dozen

Between the Lakes

Apple French Toast

1   large loaf French bread
8   extra-large eggs
3 1/2   cups milk
1/2   cup sugar
1   tablespoon vanilla extract
6   to 8 cooking apples (McIntosh or
      Cortland), peeled and sliced
1/2   cup sugar
1   tablespoon cinnamon
1   teaspoon nutmeg
1   tablespoon butter, cut into small
      pieces
      Maple syrup, heated
      Confectioners' sugar

Slice the bread 1/2 inch thick and arrange in a single layer in a greased 9×13-inch baking dish. Combine the eggs, milk, 1/2 cup sugar and vanilla in a mixing bowl and whisk for 30 seconds. Pour half the egg mixture over the bread. Arrange the apples slices over the bread to cover. Pour on the remaining egg mixture. Combine 1/2 cup sugar, cinnamon and nutmeg in a small bowl and sprinkle over the egg mixture. Dot with the butter. Chill, covered, for 8 hours. Bake at 350 degrees for 1 hour. Let stand for 10 minutes. Serve with maple syrup and confectioners' sugar.

Serves 8

Crème Brûlée French Toast

1/2   cup (1 stick) unsalted butter
1   cup packed brown sugar
2   tablespoons corn syrup
1   (8- to 9-inch) round country-style
      bread
5   eggs
1 1/2   cups half-and-half
1   teaspoon vanilla extract
1   teaspoon Grand Marnier
1/4   teaspoon salt

Melt the butter with the brown sugar and corn syrup in a saucepan over medium heat, stirring until smooth. Pour into a 9×13-inch baking dish. Cut six 1-inch thick slices from the center of the bread. Arrange the bread slices in a single layer in the baking dish. Whisk the eggs, half-and-half, vanilla, Grand Marnier and salt in a bowl. Pour over the bread. Chill, covered, for 8 to 24 hours. Bring the dish to room temperature. Bake at 350 degrees on the center rack of the oven for 35 to 40 minutes or until the toast is puffed and the edges are pale gold. Serve immediately.

Serves 6

Blueberry Pancakes

2	cups flour
1	teaspoon baking soda
1	teaspoon salt
2	tablespoons sugar
2	eggs, slightly beaten
2	cups buttermilk
2	tablespoons butter or margarine, melted
1	cup fresh or frozen blueberries, or more to taste
1	cup sugar
2	tablespoons cornstarch
1/4	teaspoon cinnamon
1	cup water
2	to 3 cups fresh or frozen blueberries
3	tablespoons lemon juice

Combine the flour, baking soda, salt and 2 tablespoons sugar in a large bowl and mix well. Combine the eggs, buttermilk and melted butter in a bowl and mix well. Add the egg mixture to the dry ingredients and mix just until moistened. Fold in 1 cup blueberries.

Combine 1 cup sugar, the cornstarch, cinnamon, water and 1 cup blueberries in a saucepan. Bring to a boil. Stir in the lemon juice.

Pour 1/4 cup batter at a time onto a hot lightly greased skillet. Cook until brown on both sides, turning once. Serve with the blueberry mixture.

Serves 6

Between the Lakes

Sour Cream Pancakes

1   cup sour cream
1   cup half-and-half
3   eggs
1   scant teaspoon salt
1   cup baking mix
1   teaspoon baking soda

Mix the sour cream, half-and-half, eggs, salt, baking mix and baking soda in a mixing bowl. Let stand in the refrigerator for 12 hours. Stir the batter well before using. Pour the batter onto a hot greased griddle making 2-inch pancakes. Cook until golden brown on both sides. Serve with melted butter and maple syrup.

Serves 4

Sunday Breakfast

    Cream cheese
1   bagel, split and toasted
2   home-grown tomato slices
    Garlic salt to taste

Spread the cream cheese on each bagel half. Top each with a tomato slice and sprinkle with garlic salt.

Serves 1

MAPLE SYRUP

Almost 50,000 gallons of maple syrup are produced in Michigan, ranking the state seventh in the country for production of this sweet, rich sap. It takes approximately 40 gallons of sap to produce one gallon of syrup. The excess water is boiled off to concentrate the sugars. A container of maple syrup can be stored on the shelf until it is ready to be used, but once opened, it should be refrigerated.

Apple Lasagna

2   cups (8 ounces) shredded Cheddar
    cheese
1   cup ricotta cheese
1   egg, lightly beaten
1/4 cup sugar
1   teaspoon almond extract
1   (20-ounce) can apple pie filling
8   lasagna noodles, cooked, drained and
    rinsed
1   (20-ounce) can apple pie filling
6   tablespoons flour
6   tablespoons packed brown sugar
1/4 cup quick-cooking oats
1/2 teaspoon cinnamon
    Dash of nutmeg
3   tablespoons margarine
1   cup sour cream
1/3 cup packed brown sugar

Mix the first 5 ingredients in a mixing bowl. Spread 1 can of pie filling in a greased 9×13-inch baking dish. Place 4 lasagna noodles over the pie filling. Spread the cheese mixture over the noodles. Top with the remaining noodles. Spread with 1 can of pie filling. Combine the flour, 6 tablespoons brown sugar, oats, cinnamon and nutmeg in a bowl. Cut in the margarine until crumbly. Sprinkle the oats mixture over the pie filling. Bake at 350 degrees for 45 minutes. Cool for 15 minutes. Mix the sour cream and 1/3 cup brown sugar in a bowl. Chill, covered, until serving time. Serve with the lasagna.

Serves 12 to 15

Baked Oatmeal

2 3/4 cups rolled oats
1/2 cup oat bran
2   teaspoons baking powder
1/2 teaspoon salt
1/2 teaspoon cinnamon
2   cups milk
1   egg, beaten
1/3 cup applesauce
1/4 cup vegetable oil
1/4 cup sugar
1/4 cup packed brown sugar
2   cups fresh blueberries or raspberries,
     or 2 cups chopped pears, apples or
     strawberries
     Plain vanilla low-fat yogurt, milk
     or cream

Combine the rolled oats, oat bran, baking powder, salt and cinnamon in a large mixing bowl. Set aside. Combine the milk, egg, applesauce, oil, sugar and brown sugar in a bowl and mix well. Add the milk mixture to the dry ingredients, stirring until combined. Spoon into a lightly greased 2-quart soufflé dish or baking dish. Bake at 400 degrees for 20 minutes. Stir the oatmeal and gently fold in the fruit. Bake for 20 minutes longer or until the top is lightly browned. Serve with yogurt.

Serves 8

Between the Lakes

Ham and Egg Bake

8   slices bread, crusts removed
     Butter
1/2   cup (2 ounces) shredded sharp Cheddar cheese
1   (4-ounce) can mushrooms, drained
2   cups cubed cooked ham
2   cups milk
3   eggs
1/2   teaspoon each salt, dry mustard and pepper

Spread the bread with butter. Cut the bread into cubes. Layer
1/2 the bread and cheese in a buttered 11/2- to 2-quart baking dish.
Add the mushrooms and ham. Layer with the remaining bread and
cheese. Combine the remaining ingredients in a mixing bowl and mix
well. Pour over the ham mixture. Chill, covered, for 12 hours. Bake at
325 degrees for 1 hour.

Serves 6

Baked Egg Roll

12   eggs
2   tablespoons flour
4   ounces cream cheese, softened
1/2   cup milk
     Dijon mustard
2   cups (8 ounces) shredded Cheddar or Colby Jack cheese
1   cup chopped ham
3/4   cup chopped red bell pepper

Mix the first 4 ingredients in a mixing bowl. Pour into a 13x18-
inch baking pan lined with parchment paper. Bake at 350 degrees for
12 to 15 minutes or until firm. Brush with mustard. Sprinkle with the
remaining ingredients. Roll up from the short side and slice. Serve
with fruit.

Serves 10 to 12

CEREAL
*The first modern
and commercial
cereal foods were
created by the
American Seventh-
day Adventists.
Strictly vegetarians,
Adventists formed
the Western Health
Reform Institute in
the 1860s. The
Institute was later
renamed the Battle
Creek Sanitarium
after its location
in Battle Creek,
Michigan. The
Adventists
manufactured,
promoted, and sold
wholesome cereals.*

Junior League of Saginaw Breakfast Eggs

6   slices bread
    Butter
6   eggs
1/2   cup white wine
1/2   cup chicken broth
1 1/2   cups milk
8   ounces shredded Gruyère cheese
1   (4-ounce) can sliced mushrooms
    Chopped parsley to taste
    Onion salt to taste
    Pepper to taste

Spread the bread with butter. Place the bread buttered-side down in a 9×12-inch baking dish. Combine the eggs, wine, chicken broth and milk in a mixing bowl and mix well. Add the cheese, mushrooms, parsley, onion salt and pepper. Pour over the bread. Chill, covered, for 2 hours. Bake at 350 degrees for 30 minutes.

Serves 4 to 6

Elegant Eggs

3   tablespoons butter
3   tablespoons flour
1   cup milk
1   (8-ounce) jar Cheez Whiz
12   hard-cooked eggs, sliced
1   (4-ounce) can sliced mushrooms, drained
    Seasoned bread crumbs
8   ounces bacon, crisp-cooked and crumbled

Melt the butter in a saucepan. Stir in the flour. Whisk in the milk. Cook until thickened, stirring constantly. Whisk in the Cheez Whiz. Place the sliced eggs and mushrooms in a greased 9×9-inch baking dish. Pour the cheese mixture over the eggs and mushrooms. Top with the bread crumbs. Bake at 350 degrees for 20 to 30 minutes. Sprinkle with the bacon.

Serves 6 to 8

Between the Lakes

Brunch Enchiladas

2   cups cubed cooked ham or chicken
1/2   cup chopped green onions
1/2   cup chopped green bell pepper
8   (7-inch) flour tortillas
1 1/2 cups (6 ounces) shredded sharp
      Cheddar cheese
4   eggs, beaten
2   cups half-and-half or milk
1   tablespoon flour
1/2   teaspoon garlic powder
1   cup (4 ounces) shredded sharp
      Cheddar cheese

Combine the ham, green onions and
bell pepper in a bowl. Spoon the ham
mixture down the center of the tortillas.
Sprinkle 3 tablespoons cheese over each
tortilla and roll up to enclose the filling.
Place seam side down in a greased
8×12-inch baking dish. Combine the eggs,
half-and-half, flour and garlic powder in
a mixing bowl and mix well. Pour over the
enchiladas. Chill, covered, for 12 hours.
Bake at 350 degrees for 45 to 50 minutes.
Sprinkle with 1 cup cheese. Bake for
3 minutes longer.

Serves 8

Sausage Ring

1   pound hot bulk pork sausage
1   pound mild bulk pork sausage
2   eggs, beaten
2   tablespoons to 3/4 cup chopped onion,
      or to taste
1 1/2 cups bread crumbs
1/4   cup chopped fresh parsley
      Scrambled eggs

Combine the hot pork sausage, mild
pork sausage, eggs, onion, bread crumbs
and parsley in a mixing bowl and mix well.
Spoon the sausage mixture into a greased
ovenproof 9-inch ring mold. Bake at 350
degrees for 20 to 30 minutes. Remove from
the oven. Drain off the drippings. Bake for
30 minutes longer. Unmold onto a heated
platter and fill the ring with scrambled eggs.

Serves 8 to 10

Morel Quiche

4	ounces lean bacon, diced	1	egg white
1	tablespoon butter	1/2	cup (2 ounces) diced
1/4	cup sliced wild onions or		Gruyère cheese
	scallions	2	cups half-and-half,
1	tablespoon butter		scalded and cooled
4	cups morel mushrooms,	3	eggs
	cleaned and dried	1/4	teaspoon salt
	Butter for sautéing	1/8	teaspoon white pepper
	Pâte Brisée (below)		Freshly grated nutmeg

Cook the bacon in a sauté pan until almost crisp. Drain the bacon and set aside. Melt 1 tablespoon butter in the sauté pan. Add the wild onions and sauté until translucent. Set aside. Melt 1 tablespoon butter in the sauté pan. Add a batch of mushrooms and sauté just until tender. Set aside. Repeat with the remaining mushrooms, adding 1 tablespoon butter for each batch. Roll the Pâte Brisée into a circle. Fit into a 9-inch pie plate, trimming and fluting the edge. Pierce with fork tines and brush with the egg white. Layer the bacon, onions and mushrooms in the pastry. Sprinkle with the cheese. Whisk the half-and-half into the eggs in a mixing bowl. Add the salt, pepper and nutmeg. Pour over the cheese. Bake at 375 degrees for 35 minutes or until the top is golden brown. Serve warm.

Serves 6 to 8

Pâte Brisée

1/2	cup (1 stick) butter,	1/2	teaspoon salt
	softened	1/2	to 3/4 cup water
2	cups sifted flour		

Lightly rub the butter into the flour and salt in a bowl with fingers, then by hand. Make a well in the flour mixture. Add the water gradually and stir with the index finger, moving to the outer edge to incorporate flour. Form into a ball and let rest for up to 2 hours.

Between the Lakes

Wild Rice Quiche

1   unbaked (9-inch) pie shell
1   tablespoon butter
1/3 cup chopped Canadian bacon
1   small onion, finely chopped
1   cup (4 ounces) shredded Gruyère or
     Monterey Jack cheese
1   cup cooked wild rice
3   eggs
1 1/2 cups half-and-half
1/2 teaspoon salt

Place pie weights or dried beans in the pie shell. Bake at 425 degrees for 5 minutes. Remove from the oven. Remove the pie weights and set aside. Melt the butter in a skillet. Add the Canadian bacon and onion and sauté until the onion is translucent. Spoon into the partially baked pie shell. Spread with the cheese and wild rice. Beat the eggs, half-and-half and salt in a small bowl. Pour over the wild rice. Bake at 350 degrees for 35 minutes or until the center is almost set. Let stand for 10 minutes before slicing.

Serves 6

Pita Sandwich

1   thin pita bread
     Honey mustard or spicy sweet mustard
     Swiss or Cheddar cheese
     Thinly sliced salami

Cut around the edges of the pita bread to split in half. Spread both sides lightly with honey mustard. Slice enough cheese with a plane to cover the bottom piece of bread. Cover the cheese with salami slices. Cover the salami with the top piece of bread. Place the sandwich on a rack in a broiler pan. Toast both sides under the broiler.

Serves 1

Hot Spiced Fruit Compote

1/4   cup (1/2 stick) butter
1/2   cup packed brown sugar
1   teaspoon curry powder
2   teaspoons cinnamon
1   teaspoon cornstarch
1   (1-pound) can pineapple chunks,
      drained
1   (1-pound) can sliced pears, drained
1   (1-pound) can sliced peaches,
      drained
1   (16-ounce) can sliced apricots,
      drained
10   maraschino cherries

Melt the butter in a small saucepan.
Add the brown sugar, curry powder,
cinnamon and cornstarch and mix well.
Set aside. Place the pineapple, pears,
peaches and apricots in a baking dish.
Add the cherries. Spoon on the butter
mixture. Bake at 325 degrees for 1 hour,
stirring occasionally.

Serves 6

No-Brainer Breakfast in a Glass

1   medium banana
6   frozen strawberries
8   seedless frozen grapes
1/2   small apple, cored
1/2   cup frozen low-fat strawberry yogurt
1 1/2 cups orange juice

Combine the banana, strawberries,
grapes, unpeeled apple, yogurt and orange
juice in a blender. Process for 1 minute or
until chopped. Purée for 30 seconds.

Serves 2

Between the Lakes

Salads and Soups

Grilled Shrimp Salad
Curried Artichoke and Shrimp Salad
Grilled Tomato Bread Salad
Crunchy Romaine Salad
Matchmaker Salad
Traverse City Dried Cherry Salad
Orange and Romaine Salad
Raspberry and Spinach Salad
Fruited Winter Slaw
Chicken Fruit Salad
Frosted Fruit Salad
Grape Salad
Frozen Spiced Peach Salad
Tomato and Peach Salad
Warm Goat Cheese Salad
Spaghetti Salad
Layered Spinach Tortellini Salad
Leprechaun Twist
Asparagus and Bell Peppers with
Balsamic Vinaigrette
Broccoli and Raisin Salad
Caprese Salad
Rice and Black Bean Salad with
Feta Cheese
Roasted Potato Salad

Creamy Dill Dressing
Green Goddess Dressing
Butternut Squash Bisque
Mushroom Bisque
Crab Bisque
Sausage Chili
Corn Chowder
Sweet Potato and Corn Chowder
with Chicken
Chicken Gumbo
Three-Bean Soup
Easy Bean and Sausage Soup
Hot Pork and Cabbage Soup
Italian Wedding Soup
Minestrone
Mexican Lime Soup
Tortilla Soup
Oysters Rockefeller Soup
with Croutons
French Onion Soup
Vichyssoise
Creamy Spinach Soup
Basil and Tomato Soup
Sizzling Rice Soup
Wild Rice Soup

Salads and Soups

Grilled Shrimp Salad

4	pounds medium shrimp, peeled and butterflied
5	teaspoons minced garlic
3	tablespoons olive oil
2	teaspoons salt
	Freshly ground pepper to taste
2	(2-ounce) cans flat anchovy fillets
1/4	cup fresh lemon juice
1/2	cup olive oil
2	tablespoons water
1/4	cup pine nuts
	Coarse salt to taste
1	teaspoon minced garlic
1	cup marinated sun-dried tomatoes, cut into large strips
1/2	cup capers
1	cup firmly packed, torn fresh basil leaves

Combine the shrimp, 5 teaspoons garlic, 3 tablespoons olive oil, 2 teaspoons salt and pepper in a large bowl and toss to coat the shrimp. Chill for 1 hour.

Place the undrained anchovies and lemon juice in a food processor fitted with a steel blade. Purée by pulsing 4 or 5 times. Add 1/2 cup olive oil in a fine stream processing constantly. Add 2 tablespoons water and process well. The dressing should be a medium-thin consistency so add a few drops of water if necessary. Remove the dressing and set aside.

Spread the pine nuts in a single layer in a roasting pan. Bake at 400 degrees for 6 minutes or until the nuts turn golden brown. Sprinkle with coarse salt and set aside.

Arrange the shrimp on a fine-mesh grid. Grill for 5 minutes per side or until the shrimp turn opaque.

Place the shrimp in a large bowl. Add 1 teaspoon garlic, toasted pine nuts and anchovy dressing and mix well. Add the sun-dried tomatoes, capers and basil and toss well to mix.

Serves 6

Curried Artichoke and Shrimp Salad

1	(8-ounce) package chicken-flavored Rice-A-Roni
1	(6-ounce) jar marinated artichoke hearts
1	(4-ounce) can shrimp, or 8 ounces cooked shrimp, cut into pieces
2	green onions, chopped
8	black olives, sliced
3/4	cup mayonnaise
1/2	teaspoon curry powder

Prepare the rice mix according to package directions using only 1 tablespoon of butter or margarine to brown the rice. Cool the rice to room temperature. Drain and chop the artichoke hearts, reserving 1 tablespoon marinade. Stir the artichoke hearts, shrimp, green onions and olives into the rice. Combine the mayonnaise, the reserved artichoke marinade and curry powder in a bowl. Stir the mayonnaise dressing into the rice. Spoon the rice mixture into a salad bowl. Chill, covered, for 8 to 12 hours. Garnish with lemon slices and parsley sprigs before serving.

Serves 6

Between the Lakes

Grilled Tomato Bread Salad

4	cups French or peasant bread, cut into 1-inch cubes
2	tablespoons olive oil
1	teaspoon thyme
	Salt and freshly ground pepper to taste
3	red onions, peeled and cut crosswise into 1/2-inch slices
1	tablespoon olive oil
8	plum tomatoes
1	tablespoon olive oil
1	cucumber, peeled, halved lengthwise and cut into 1-inch pieces
1/2	cup fresh basil leaves, slivered
2	tablespoons olive oil
2	tablespoons red wine vinegar

Place the bread cubes in a large bowl. Drizzle with 2 tablespoons olive oil. Add the thyme, salt and pepper and toss well. Set aside. Brush the onion slices lightly on both sides with 1 tablespoon olive oil and place on a grill rack. Grill 3 inches from medium-hot coals for 5 minutes per side. Remove the onions to a plate and set aside. Place 4 plum tomatoes lengthwise on each of 2 metal skewers. Brush the tomatoes lightly with 1 tablespoon olive oil and place on a grill rack. Grill for 5 minutes or until hot but still slightly firm, turning to heat all sides. Remove the tomatoes to a plate and set aside. Thread the bread cubes onto skewers, leaving space between the cubes. Place the skewers on a grill rack. Grill for 1 1/2 minutes on each of 4 sides. Remove the bread to a bowl. Cut the onions into quarters and add to the bowl. Cut the tomatoes into quarters using a serrated knife and add to the bowl. Add the cucumber and basil. Add the remaining 2 tablespoons olive oil and vinegar and toss well. Adjust the seasonings and serve immediately.

Serves 6

Crunchy Romaine Salad

CHERRIES

Michigan is the nation's number one cherry producing state yielding 70 to 75 percent of all tart cherries grown. Cherries are high in potassium and Vitamin C and low in fat and sodium. Their outstanding nutritional value is equal to and often higher than that of many other fruits.

1/4	cup (1/2 stick) unsalted butter
1	(3-ounce) package ramen noodles, crumbled, without flavor packet
1	cup walnuts, chopped
1	head romaine lettuce, torn into bite-size pieces
1	bunch broccoli florets, chopped
4	green onions, chopped
1	cup vegetable oil
1/2	cup sugar
1/2	cup wine vinegar
1	tablespoon soy sauce
	Salt and pepper to taste

Melt the butter in a saucepan. Add the noodles and walnuts. Brown the noodle mixture, stirring often. Remove and cool on paper towels. Line a salad bowl with the romaine lettuce leaves. Add the noodles, walnuts, broccoli and green onions. Whisk together the oil, sugar, vinegar, soy sauce, salt and pepper in a small bowl. Add enough dressing to coat the salad and toss to coat.

Note: Any remaining dressing can be stored in an airtight container in the refrigerator.

Serves 8 to 10

Between the Lakes

Matchmaker Salad

2   pounds frozen peas or green beans
1   large head lettuce, torn into
    bite-size pieces
1   bunch carrots, peeled and grated
1   red onion, sliced
1   (16-ounce) can pineapple tidbits,
    drained
1   pound seedless green grapes
2   cups mayonnaise
8   ounces bacon, crisp-cooked and
    crumbled

Cook the peas using the package
directions; drain. Layer half the lettuce,
peas, carrots, onion, pineapple and grapes
in a large glass bowl in the order listed.
Spread on half the mayonnaise. Repeat the
layers, spreading the remaining 1 cup
mayonnaise to the edge. Sprinkle the bacon
over the top. Chill, covered, for at least
6 hours before serving. Toss and serve.

Serves 12

Traverse City Dried Cherry Salad

1/2   cup raspberry vinegar
1/2   cup olive oil
1/2   cup vegetable oil
1/2   cup maple syrup
2   tablespoons Dijon mustard
2   tablespoons fresh tarragon leaves
1/2   teaspoon salt
3   heads red leaf lettuce
1/4   cup crumbled blue cheese
12   red onion rings
      Dried cherries or strawberries to taste
1   tablespoon pine nuts, lightly sautéed

Combine the vinegar, olive oil, vegetable
oil, maple syrup, mustard, tarragon and salt
in a small bowl and mix well. Place the
lettuce in a large salad bowl. Add 3/4 cup
dressing and toss the lettuce by hand to
mix. Top with the blue cheese, onion rings,
dried cherries and pine nuts.

Note: The remaining dressing can
be stored in an airtight container in
the refrigerator.

Serves 8 to 10

Orange and Romaine Salad

1   envelope garlic and herb salad
     dressing mix
1/4   cup white balsamic vinegar
3   tablespoons water
1/2   cup olive oil
3   heads romaine lettuce
2   (11-ounce) cans mandarin oranges,
     drained
1/3   cup toasted pine nuts
4   ounces Gorgonzola cheese, crumbled

Combine the salad dressing mix, balsamic vinegar, water and olive oil in a bowl according to package directions. Set aside. Chop, rinse and dry the lettuce. Remove to a large salad bowl. Add the oranges, pine nuts and cheese. Drizzle with the dressing or serve on the side.

Serves 4 to 6

Raspberry and Spinach Salad

2   tablespoons vinegar
2   tablespoons raspberry jam
1/3   cup vegetable oil
8   cups spinach
3/4   cup macadamia nuts, coarsely
     chopped
1   cup fresh raspberries
3   kiwifruit, peeled and thinly sliced

Combine the vinegar and jam in a blender or small bowl. Add the oil in a fine stream processing constantly at high speed until blended. Rinse and dry the spinach; remove stems. Tear into a shallow salad bowl. Add half the macadamia nuts, half the raspberries and half the kiwifruit. Toss with the salad dressing. Top with the remaining macadamia nuts, raspberries and kiwifruit.

Serves 8

Between the Lakes

Fruited Winter Slaw

1 1/3 cups vegetable or peanut oil
1/2 cup cider vinegar
1/2 cup lemon juice
1/4 cup honey
1/2 teaspoon ground ginger
1 garlic clove, peeled and halved
2 teaspoons salt
1/2 teaspoon ground pepper
1 small head red cabbage, shredded (1 1/2 pounds)
1 small head green cabbage, shredded (1 1/2 pounds)
1 small onion, shredded
   Salt and pepper to taste
   Sliced dried apricots to taste
   Sliced dried bananas to taste
   Cashews to taste

Combine the oil, vinegar, lemon juice, honey, ginger, garlic, remaining salt and pepper in a jar with a tight-fitting lid and shake well. Chill for 2 to 12 hours. Remove and let stand at room temperature for 15 minutes. Remove the garlic and shake well.

Layer the red and green cabbage in a large salad bowl. Add the onion, salt and pepper to taste. Arrange the apricots, bananas and cashews in the center.

Pour the honey mixture over the vegetables and toss well.

Serves 10 to 12

Chicken Fruit Salad

4   cups chopped cooked chicken
1/2 cup chopped celery
1   (20-ounce) can crushed pineapple,
      well drained
3/4 cup chopped walnuts
3/4 cup maraschino cherries, well drained
      and halved
3/4 cup red seedless grapes
1/2 cup mayonnaise
1/2 cup whipped topping

Combine the chicken, celery, pineapple, walnuts, cherries and grapes in a large salad bowl. Fold in the mayonnaise and whipped topping. Cover and refrigerate for several hours. Adjust the mayonnaise and whipped topping before serving.

Serves 4

Frosted Fruit Salad

2   (3-ounce) packages lemon gelatin
2   cups hot water
2   cups ginger ale
2   cups miniature marshmallows
1   cup crushed pineapple
3   bananas, sliced
1/2 cup sugar
2   tablespoons flour
1   egg, beaten
1   cup pineapple juice
2   tablespoons butter
1/2 cup whipped cream
      Shredded Cheddar cheese

Dissolve the gelatin in the hot water in a heatproof bowl. Add the ginger ale. Chill until partially set. Fold in the marshmallows, pineapple and bananas. Pour into a serving bowl. Chill until firm.

Combine the sugar, flour, egg and pineapple juice in a small saucepan. Cook until thickened, stirring occasionally. Add the butter and remove from heat to cool. Fold into the whipped cream in a large bowl. Spread over the fruit mixture and sprinkle with the cheese.

Serves 8 to 10

Between the Lakes

Grape Salad

1   (8-ounce) package cream cheese, softened
1   cup sour cream
1/2 cup sugar
1   teaspoon vanilla extract
4   pounds green grapes or red and green grapes
     Brown sugar to taste
1/2 cup chopped walnuts

Beat the cream cheese, sour cream, sugar and vanilla together in a large bowl until smooth. Add the grapes and toss to coat. Sprinkle lightly with brown sugar and top with walnuts.

Serves 16

Frozen Spiced Peach Salad

1   (30-ounce) jar spiced peaches
1   (3-ounce) package cream cheese, softened
1/4 cup sugar
1   tablespoon lemon juice
1   cup miniature marshmallows
1/2 cup chopped pecans
2/3 cup evaporated milk, frozen (crystals around the edge)
     Lettuce leaves

Drain the peaches, reserving half the liquid. Chop the peaches. Beat the cream cheese and sugar in a mixing bowl until smooth. Beat in the reserved peach liquid and lemon juice. Fold in the peaches, marshmallows and pecans. Beat the evaporated milk in a mixing bowl until stiff peaks form. Fold into the cream cheese mixture. Pour into a 7×11-inch pan. Cover and freeze. Cut into squares and serve on lettuce leaves.

Serves 10 to 12

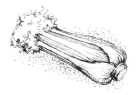

CELERY

Michigan was the birthplace of the nation's celery industry. When choosing celery, look for green, crisp, and thick stalks. Celery stalks that are smooth inside and have a glossy surface will taste best. If left uncovered, celery will lose moisture. To replace the moisture, place celery in a water bath.

Tomato and Peach Salad

1   ripe tomato, peeled, seeded and chopped
1   ripe peach, peeled and diced
1   teaspoon balsamic vinegar
1   teaspoon mild olive oil
     Dash of salt

Combine the tomato and peach in a salad bowl and toss gently. Add the vinegar, olive oil and salt and toss gently. Let stand at least 5 minutes before serving, stirring occasionally.

Serves 2

Warm Goat Cheese Salad

2 1/2 tablespoons balsamic vinegar
1/2   teaspoon Dijon mustard
1/2   cup olive oil
     Salt and pepper to taste
1   baguette
8   ounces soft goat cheese
6   ounces (6 cups) mesclun

Whisk the vinegar and mustard together in a bowl. Slowly add the oil in a steady stream, whisking constantly. Add the salt and pepper. Cut the baquette into 12 slices 1/2 inch thick. Cut the goat cheese into slices 1/4 inch thick. Place the baguette slices on a baking sheet. Top with the goat cheese. Broil 6 inches from the heat source for 2 to 3 minutes or until the bread is golden brown and the cheese starts to melt. Place mesclun in a large bowl. Add the dressing and toss to combine. Place the mesclun on 4 salad plates. Arrange 3 toasts over each serving.

Serves 4

Between the Lakes

Spaghetti Salad

1   tablespoon vegetable oil
16   ounces spaghetti, broken into quarters
1/2   cucumber, chopped
1   bunch radishes, sliced
1   bunch green onions, sliced
1 1/2 teaspoons salt
1   teaspoon sugar
3/4   teaspoon pepper
1/2   teaspoon celery salt
1   large pinch of oregano
4   hard-cooked eggs, sliced
4   cups mayonnaise
2/3   cup sour cream
1   cup milk or half-and-half
1/4   cup Durkee sauce
1   teaspoon Dijon mustard

Bring a large pan of water to a boil.
Add the oil and spaghetti and cook until al
dente. Drain and remove to a serving bowl.
Add the cucumber, radishes, green onions,
salt, sugar, pepper, celery salt, oregano
and eggs.

Combine the mayonnaise, sour cream,
milk, Durkee sauce and mustard in a large
bowl and mix well. Stir 2 1/2 cups of the
mayonnaise mixture into vegetable mixture.
Chill, covered, for 8 to 12 hours.

Note: Leftover dressing can be stored in
an airtight container in the refrigerator for
up to 2 days.

Serves 8

Layered Spinach Tortellini Salad

1   (9-ounce) package refrigerator
      cheese tortellini
6   cups torn baby spinach leaves
2   cups red cabbage, shredded
1   cup cherry tomatoes, halved
1/2   cup sliced green onions
1   (8-ounce) bottle ranch salad dressing
8   slices bacon, crisp-cooked and
      crumbled

Cook the tortellini according to the
package directions. Drain and rinse under
cold water; drain well. Layer the spinach,
cabbage, tortellini, tomatoes and green
onions in a glass bowl. Pour the dressing
evenly over the top. Sprinkle with the
bacon. Chill, covered, until serving time.

Serves 6 to 8

Leprechaun Twist

1/2 cup sour cream
1/4 cup mayonnaise
2 tablespoons half-and-half or milk
3 tablespoons tarragon vinegar or wine vinegar
2 tablespoons olive oil
1 1/2 teaspoons sugar
1 teaspoon salt
1/4 teaspoon freshly ground pepper
1 teaspoon crushed tarragon
4 garlic cloves, minced
8 ounces rotini or gemelli (strands of spaghetti twisted together)
2 cups shredded cooked corned beef
1 1/2 cups coarsely shredded cabbage
1/2 cup shredded carrots
1/2 cup thinly sliced celery
1/2 cup chopped green bell pepper
1/2 cup chopped green onions

Combine the sour cream, mayonnaise, half-and-half, vinegar, olive oil, sugar, salt, pepper, tarragon and garlic in a food processor. Process until the garlic is puréed and set aside. Bring a large pan of water to a boil. Add the rotini and cook until al dente. Drain and rinse under cold water; drain well. Remove the rotini to a bowl. Mix with 1/4 cup of the garlic mixture. Chill in the refrigerator. Add the corned beef, cabbage, carrots, celery, bell pepper and green onions and toss gently. Add 1/2 cup of the garlic mixture and mix well. Chill, covered, until serving time. Stir in the remaining garlic mixture just before serving.

Serves 6

Between the Lakes

Asparagus and Bell Peppers with Balsamic Vinaigrette

2 to 3 cups cooked asparagus pieces sliced 1 1/2 inches on the diagonal
1/2 yellow or red bell pepper, cut into strips 1 1/2 inches long and 1/8 inch thick
2 tablespoons balsamic vinegar or sherry vinegar
1 to 2 tablespoons canola oil
1 teaspoon Dijon mustard
   Dash of salt
2 tablespoons crumbled feta cheese, or to taste

Combine the asparagus and bell pepper in a salad bowl. Whisk together the vinegar, oil, mustard and salt. Pour the vinaigrette over the asparagus mixture and toss to coat. Sprinkle with the cheese and mix gently.

Variation: Substitute cooked green beans and halved grape tomatoes for the asparagus and bell pepper.

Serves 4

ASPARAGUS
Michigan ranks third in the nation for asparagus production. Keep fresh asparagus clean, cold, and covered. Trim the stem end about 1/4 inch and wash in warm water. Place in moisture-proof wrapping. Refrigerate and use within 2 or 3 days. To maintain freshness, stand in two inches of cold water.

Broccoli and Raisin Salad

1   cup mayonnaise
1/2   cup sugar
2 1/2   tablespoons vinegar
4   cups broccoli florets
2   slices bacon, crisp-cooked and crumbled
1   cup raisins
1/2   cup chopped pecans
1/2   cup chopped red onion

Combine the mayonnaise, sugar and vinegar in a large bowl and mix well. Add the broccoli, bacon, raisins, pecans and red onion and mix well. Serve immediately or chill, covered, for several hours.

Note: To make this salad in advance, stir in the pecans and raisins just before serving.

Serves 4

Caprese Salad

3   pints small cherry tomatoes
8   ounces fresh mozzarella cheese, diced
2/3   ounce fresh basil, chopped
1/3   cup balsamic vinegar
1/2   cup extra-virgin olive oil
   Salt and pepper to taste

Mix the tomatoes, cheese and basil in a large bowl. Whisk together the vinegar and olive oil in a small bowl and pour over the tomato mixture. Add the salt and pepper. Toss gently by hand.

Serves 8 to 10

Between the Lakes

Rice and Black Bean Salad with Feta Cheese

1   (15-ounce) can black beans, drained and rinsed
1 1/2   cups chopped tomatoes
1 1/2   cups cooked rice
1   cup (4 ounces) crumbled feta cheese
1/2   cup chopped celery
1/2   cup sliced green onions
1/2   cup Italian salad dressing
2   tablespoons chopped fresh cilantro or parsley

Combine the beans, tomatoes, rice, cheese, celery and green onions in a salad bowl. Add the Italian salad dressing and mix gently. Stir in the cilantro. Chill, covered, until serving time.

Serves 6

Roasted Potato Salad

2   pounds potatoes, quartered
Olive oil
Salt and pepper to taste
10   garlic cloves, minced
3/4   cup mayonnaise
2   tablespoons whole-grain mustard
Juice of 1/2 lemon
1/4   cup fresh cilantro, chopped
1/2   red onion, sliced

Toss the potatoes with a drizzle of olive oil in a bowl. Season with salt and pepper. Place the potatoes on a baking sheet. Bake at 400 degrees until fork tender. Combine the garlic, mayonnaise, mustard, lemon juice, salt and pepper in a bowl and mix well. Add the cilantro, onion and roasted potatoes and mix well. Serve hot or cold.

Serves 8

Creamy Dill Dressing

1   cup buttermilk
3   tablespoons mayonnaise
1/4 cup chopped fresh dill weed, or
     4 teaspoons dried dill weed
3   tablespoons chopped fresh chives, or
     1 tablespoon dried chives
1   tablespoon chopped fresh parsley, or
     1 teaspoon dried parsley
1   tablespoon lemon juice
1   teaspoon Dijon mustard
     Salt and pepper to taste

Combine the buttermilk, mayonnaise, dill weed, chives, parsley, lemon juice, mustard, salt and pepper in a blender and process until the herbs are minced. Chill, covered, at least 1 hour or up to 4 days before serving. Serve over salad greens or sliced, seeded cucumbers.

Makes about 1 1/2 cups

Green Goddess Dressing

1   cup mayonnaise
1   garlic clove, crushed
3   tablespoons finely chopped onion
1/3 cup chopped fresh parsley
1/2 cup sour cream
1   tablespoon lemon juice, or
     3 tablespoons vinegar
     Salt and pepper to taste

Combine the mayonnaise, garlic, onion, parsley, sour cream, lemon juice, salt and pepper in a blender and process until the vegetables are puréed. Remove the dressing to a container with an airtight lid and refrigerate for up to 4 days.

Makes about 1 3/4 cups

Between the Lakes

Butternut Squash Bisque

1/2 cup (1 stick) unsalted butter
1   cup diced onion
1/2 cup flour
5 1/2 cups chicken stock or broth
5   cups peeled and diced butternut squash (3 pounds)
1   cup dry white wine
3   bay leaves
1   cup half-and-half
     Salt and pepper to taste
1   (8-ounce) package imitation crab meat (optional)

Melt the butter in a large heavy saucepan over medium-low heat. Add the onion. Sauté until translucent, stirring occasionally. Add the flour. Cook for 3 minutes, stirring constantly. Add the chicken stock. Cook until thickened, stirring constantly. Add the squash, wine and bay leaves. Simmer for 15 to 20 minutes or until the squash is very tender. Stir in the half-and-half, salt and pepper. Remove the bay leaves. Purée the soup in the blender. Return to the saucepan and cook until heated through. Add the crab meat.

Note: If desired make the soup a day in advance and refrigerate. Reheat before serving.

Serves 8

Mushroom Bisque

4 1/4 cups mushrooms (see note)
1/2   cup (1 stick) butter
3   shallots, chopped
1   garlic clove, minced
1   cup sherry
2   cups chicken broth
1   cup heavy cream
     Salt and pepper to taste
     Chicken base to taste
1   tablespoon minced chives (optional)

Separate the mushroom caps from the stems. Mince the caps in a food processor by pulsing 4 or 5 times. Set aside. Mince the stems in a food processor by pulsing 4 or 5 times. Melt the butter in a large saucepan. Sauté the shallots and garlic. Add the mushroom caps, stems and sherry. Simmer for 15 minutes. Add the chicken broth. Simmer for 30 minutes. Strain the broth into a saucepan, reserving the mushrooms. Cook the broth over high heat until reduced by 1/3. Stir the mushrooms into the broth. Add the heavy cream. Cook until heated through, stirring constantly. Add the salt, pepper and chicken base. Sprinkle with chives.

Note: Use white, oyster, shiitake or portobello mushrooms in any combination. If using shiitake mushrooms discard the stems.

Serves 6

Crab Bisque

1   (10-ounce) can green pea soup
2   (10-ounce) cans tomato soup
2   cups half-and-half
1   teaspoon sherry
1   (6-ounce) can crab meat
      Chopped parsley
      Homemade croutons

Combine the green pea soup, tomato soup, half-and-half, sherry and crab meat in a large saucepan. Warm over low heat stirring occasionally. Do not let the soup boil. Sprinkle with parsley and serve with croutons.

Serves 8

Sausage Chili

1   pound ground beef
1   pound bulk pork sausage
1   cup chopped green bell pepper
1   large onion, chopped
1   cup chopped celery
1   (15-ounce) can kidney beans
1   (15-ounce) can pinto beans
1   (6-ounce) can tomato paste
4   cups stewed tomatoes
3   garlic cloves, minced
2   teaspoons salt
1/4   cup packed brown sugar
      Shredded cheese
      Finely chopped onion

Brown the ground beef and sausage in a large skillet, stirring until crumbly; drain. Remove to a large pot. Add the bell pepper, onion, celery, kidney beans, pinto beans, tomato paste, stewed tomatoes, garlic, salt and brown sugar. Cook over low heat for 1 hour or longer. Serve with the shredded cheese and onion.

Serves 8 to 10

Corn Chowder

2	potatoes, diced
3	slices bacon, cut into small pieces
1/4	cup minced onion
2	(14-ounce) cans cream-style corn
1	cup chicken stock
1	(12-ounce) can evaporated milk, or 2 cups half-and-half
2	cups whole milk
	Salt to taste
1/4	teaspoon nutmeg
	Finely chopped fresh parsley

*B*oil the potatoes in a small amount of water in a large saucepan until almost soft. Do not drain. Set aside. Cook the bacon in a skillet over low heat until crisp. Remove the bacon. Add the onion. Sauté in the bacon drippings. Add the bacon and onion to the potatoes. Add the corn, chicken stock, evaporated milk, whole milk, salt and nutmeg. Simmer for 10 minutes. Sprinkle with the parsley.

Serves 6

Between the Lakes

Sweet Potato and Corn Chowder with Chicken

6   slices bacon, finely chopped
1/2   onion, chopped
1/4   cup (1/2 stick) butter
1   teaspoon basil
1   teaspoon thyme
1/2   cup flour
2   cups frozen corn kernels
1   red bell pepper, chopped
1   pound sweet potatoes, diced and blanched
1   cup water
6   cups chicken broth
4   cups chopped cooked chicken
1 1/2 cups milk
1   teaspoon salt
1/4   teaspoon pepper
1   tablespoon chopped parsley

Place the bacon in a saucepan and cook over medium-high heat until crisp-cooked. Drain off most of the drippings. Add the onion, butter, basil and thyme to the remaining drippings. Cook until the onion is soft. Add the flour and mix well. Stir in the corn, bell pepper and sweet potatoes. Sauté for 5 minutes. Add the water, chicken broth and chicken. Bring to a boil. Add the milk, salt and pepper. Cook until thickened, stirring constantly. Stir in the parsley.

Serves 15

CORN

Most Michigan field corn is harvested for livestock feed; however, new uses are continually being developed, including the production of biodegradable plastic bags and disposable diapers. The first large-scale ethanol production facility was recently built in Michigan. The plant distills corn for fuel-grade alcohol, which is then blended with gasoline. Corn is also used for food products such as cornmeal, oil, syrup, and breakfast cereals.

Chicken Gumbo

2 tablespoons vegetable oil
1 (2-pound) chicken, cut up
8 cups chicken stock
1 teaspoon paprika
1 bay leaf
2 garlic cloves, minced
2 tablespoons vegetable oil
1/2 cup chopped onion
1/2 cup chopped celery
1/2 cup chopped green bell pepper
4 ounces lean cooked ham
2 tablespoons flour
2 cups diced canned tomatoes
1/4 cup chopped fresh parsley
3/4 teaspoon thyme
1/4 teaspoon ground cloves
1/2 teaspoon allspice
1/4 teaspoon cumin
1 teaspoon paprika
Salt and pepper to taste
1 teaspoon grated lemon zest
1 cup frozen corn kernels
1 (10-ounce) package frozen sliced okra
Worcestershire sauce to taste
Tabasco sauce to taste
Cooked rice

Heat 2 tablespoons oil in a large saucepan. Add the chicken and brown on both sides. Add the chicken stock, 1 teaspoon paprika, bay leaf and garlic. Cover and bring to a boil. Reduce the heat and simmer for 1 hour or until the chicken is tender. Remove the chicken, cool and cut into small pieces. Set aside. Remove and discard the bay leaf. Reserve the broth.

Heat 2 tablespoons oil in a deep skillet. Brown the onion, celery, bell pepper and ham in the oil. Sprinkle with the flour. Cook for 3 minutes, stirring constantly. Add the tomatoes, parsley, thyme, cloves, allspice, cumin, 1 teaspoon paprika, salt, pepper, lemon zest and 1 cup of the reserved broth. Simmer for 10 minutes. Add the remaining broth. Cover and simmer for 1 hour. Add the chicken, corn and okra. Cook until heated through. Adjust the salt and pepper. Add the Worcestershire sauce and Tabasco sauce. Serve in bowls over rice.

Serves 8 to 10

Between the Lakes

Three-Bean Soup

1   tablespoon vegetable oil or butter
1 1/2 teaspoons chopped garlic
1   cup chopped carrots
1   cup chopped zucchini
1   cup chopped celery
1   (28-ounce) can tomatoes, cut up
3   cups water
1   (6-ounce) can tomato paste
1   teaspoon chili powder
1   tablespoon Dijon mustard
1   teaspoon basil
1   teaspoon oregano
1/2   teaspoon cumin
1/2   teaspoon pepper
1   (15-ounce) can each kidney beans, black-eyed peas, garbanzo beans and whole kernel corn, drained
      Grated Parmesan cheese

Heat the oil in a skillet. Add the garlic, carrots, zucchini and celery and sauté just until tender. Remove the vegetables to a soup pot. Add the tomatoes, water, tomato paste, chili powder, mustard, basil, oregano, cumin, pepper, kidney beans, black-eyed peas, garbanzo beans and corn. Bring to a boil. Reduce the heat and simmer, covered, for 30 minutes. Sprinkle with the cheese.

Serves 12

Easy Bean and Sausage Soup

1   tablespoon olive oil
1/2   onion, chopped, or to taste
1   pound smoked sausage, cut into cubes
1   garlic clove (optional)
2   (15-ounce) cans navy beans
1   (15-ounce) can black beans, drained
1   (14-ounce) can chicken broth
1/2   cup mild, medium or hot tomato salsa
1   to 2 teaspoons dried cilantro

Heat the olive oil in a heavy 3- or 4-quart saucepan. Add the onion. Sauté over medium heat for 2 to 3 minutes or until soft. Add the sausage, garlic, navy beans, black beans, chicken broth, salsa and cilantro. Bring the mixture to a boil. Reduce the heat and simmer for 10 to 15 minutes.

Note: If desired, add more broth for a thinner soup. Add leftover chopped cooked chicken or turkey and garnish with a sprig of fresh cilantro.

Serves 4 or 5

Hot Pork and Cabbage Soup

1   pound pork, cut into bite-size pieces
1   potato, peeled and chopped
2   ribs celery, chopped
1   onion, chopped
1   (16-ounce) package coleslaw with carrots
4   chicken bouillon cubes
4   cups water
1   (28-ounce) can tomatoes, chopped
1/4 cup packed brown sugar
1   teaspoon crushed red pepper flakes
1/2 teaspoon salt

Combine the pork, potato, celery, onion, coleslaw with carrots, bouillon cubes, water, tomatoes, brown sugar, red pepper flakes and salt in a large saucepan. Bring to a boil. Reduce the heat to low and simmer for about 1 hour or until the pork is cooked through and the potato is tender.

Serves 6 to 8

Italian Wedding Soup

1   pound Italian sausage, casings removed
1/2 large onion, chopped
1   green bell pepper, chopped
2   garlic cloves, minced
1   (28-ounce) can Italian-style tomatoes, chopped with liquid
3   (14-ounce) cans beef broth
1/2 teaspoon basil
2   cups cooked farfalle (bows), conchiglie (shells) or ditalini (short macaroni tubes)
1   medium zucchini, peeled and shredded
3   tablespoons chopped fresh parsley
     Grated Parmesan cheese to taste

Brown the sausage in a large skillet, stirring until crumbly; drain. Add the onion, bell pepper and garlic. Sauté until the vegetables are tender. Stir in the tomatoes, beef broth and basil. Simmer for 30 minutes. Stir in the farfalle, zucchini and parsley. Simmer for 15 minutes. Serve with the cheese.

Serves 8

Between the Lakes

Minestrone

1 cup pinto beans, sorted and rinsed
8 cups chicken stock
8 ounces bacon, chopped
1 large onion, chopped
1 garlic clove, minced
1 carrot, shredded
1 rib celery, diced
1 potato, cubed
  Olive oil
1 cup shredded spinach
1/4 cup parsley
1 1/2 tablespoons salt, or to taste
1 1/2 teaspoons basil
1/2 cup broken spaghetti
  Salt and pepper to taste
  Grated Parmesan cheese to taste

Soak the beans in water to cover in a bowl for 8 to 12 hours; drain. Combine the beans and chicken stock in a large pot. Bring to a boil and reduce the heat to low. Simmer for 1 hour or until tender. Place the bacon in a skillet and cook over medium-high heat until crisp-cooked. Add the onion, garlic, carrot, celery and potato and sauté until lightly browned, adding a small amount of olive oil to prevent the vegetables from sticking if necessary. Add the bacon mixture to the beans. Stir in the spinach, parsley, 1 1/2 tablespoons salt and basil. Simmer for 30 minutes. Add the spaghetti and cook for 30 minutes longer. Season with salt and pepper to taste. Serve with cheese and a drizzle of olive oil.

Serves 8 to 10

BEANS
The bean plays an important role in feeding today's world. This Michigan specialty is the highest source of protein available after meat. Beans also have more fiber than any other unprocessed food. They are low in sodium and fat and high in calcium, phosphorus, potassium, thiamine, and niacin. Beans reduce blood cholesterol levels and their low amounts of sodium and fat protect against heart disease.

Mexican Lime Soup

2   tablespoons olive oil
6   garlic cloves, chopped
6   small boneless chicken breasts, cut into 1/2-inch strips
1 1/2 teaspoons oregano
    Salt and pepper to taste
9   cups chicken broth
1/3 cup lime juice
1 1/2 cups broken tortilla chips
2   avocados, sliced
3   tomatoes, chopped
3   green onions, sliced
    Minced jalapeño chiles
    Chopped fresh cilantro
    Lime slices

Heat the olive oil in a large heavy saucepan over medium heat. Add the garlic and sauté for 20 seconds. Add the chicken strips, oregano, salt and pepper. Sauté for 3 minutes. Add the chicken broth and lime juice. Cook over high heat until the broth comes to a simmer. Reduce the heat to medium-low and simmer for 8 minutes or until the chicken is cooked through. Adjust the salt and pepper to taste. Place 3 tablespoons tortilla chips in each of 8 large soup bowls. Ladle the soup into the bowls. Top with the avocados, tomatoes, green onions, jalapeño chiles, cilantro and lime slices.

Serves 8

Tortilla Soup

1/4 cup vegetable oil
1 onion, chopped
2 fresh jalapeño chiles, seeded and chopped
4 garlic cloves, minced
2 (14-ounce) cans stewed tomatoes
2 (10-ounce) cans diced tomatoes with green chiles
2 (10-ounce) cans beef consommé
2 (10-ounce) cans chicken broth
2 (10-ounce) cans tomato soup
3 cups water
2 teaspoons cumin
1/2 teaspoon crushed red pepper flakes
2 cups shredded cooked chicken
1 (9-ounce) bag tortilla chips, broken
1 bunch cilantro, chopped
1 cup (4 ounces) shredded Monterey Jack cheese
  with peppers

Heat the oil in a Dutch oven. Add the onion, jalapeño chiles and garlic. Sauté until tender. Add the stewed tomatoes, diced tomatoes with green chiles, beef consommé, chicken broth, tomato soup, water, cumin, red pepper flakes and chicken. Bring to a boil and reduce the heat. Simmer, covered, for 1 hour. Stir in most of the tortilla chips just before serving. Top each serving with additional tortilla chips, cilantro and cheese.

Serves 12

Oysters Rockefeller Soup with Croutons

4   slices bacon, finely chopped
1   small onion, finely chopped
2   teaspoons minced garlic
1   pint oysters with liquor
4   cups heavy cream
1   pound fresh spinach
4   teaspoons salt
2   teaspoons white pepper
16   (1/4-inch-thick) slices French bread
1   large garlic clove, peeled and crushed
1/2   cup (2 ounces) shredded Gruyère cheese

Place the bacon in a large heavy stockpot and cook over medium-high heat until crisp-cooked, stirring constantly. Add the onion and cook for 5 minutes. Add the garlic and cook for 1 minute, stirring constantly. Add the undrained oysters and cream. Bring the mixture to a boil; remove from the heat. Purée the oyster mixture in a blender. Rinse and dry the spinach. Remove the stems. Add the spinach to the blender in batches and purée. Add the salt and white pepper.

Place the bread on a baking sheet. Broil until the bread is brown and toasted, turning over once. Rub 1 side of the bread with garlic. Top with the cheese. Broil 6 inches from the heat source until the cheese melts. Ladle the soup mixture into soup bowls. Top each serving with 2 croutons.

Serves 8

Between the Lakes

French Onion Soup

1/2   cup (1 stick) butter
3   large Vidalia onions
1   tablespoon sugar
1   teaspoon ginger
1/2   cup dry sherry
1/3   cup flour
4   (14-ounce) cans beef broth
     Garlic French baguette, sliced
     Shredded Gruyère, fontina, Swiss
     or provolone cheese

Melt the butter in a large stockpot. Add the onions. Cook for 20 minutes or until lightly browned. Add the sugar and cook until browned, stirring constantly. Stir in the ginger. Add the sherry and simmer for 5 minutes. Sprinkle with the flour. Cook for 1 minute, stirring constantly. Add the beef broth. Cook until the mixture comes to a boil and is thickened, stirring constantly. Reduce the heat and simmer for 25 minutes. Place a baguette slice in the bottom of each bowl. Ladle the soup over the baguette slice and cover with cheese. Place the soup bowls on a baking sheet. Broil 6 inches from the heat source for about 10 minutes or until the cheese melts and browns around the edges.

Note: If desired prepare the soup in advance. Chill, covered, for 12 hours. Reheat the soup. Assemble with the baguette and cheese and broil just before serving.

Serves 6

Vichyssoise

4   leeks or 3 onions
2 1/2   cups diced peeled potatoes
2   cups chicken broth
2   tablespoons minced fresh chives
1   tablespoon butter or margarine
1/4   teaspoon paprika
2   cups milk
1   cup heavy cream
1/4   teaspoon pepper
2   teaspoons salt
     Chopped fresh chives to taste
     Paprika to taste

Trim the leeks, leaving the whites and about 3 inches of the green tops. Cut the leeks into fine pieces. Combine the leeks, potatoes and enough water to cover in a saucepan. Boil until tender; drain. Purée the leeks and potatoes in a blender. Add the chicken broth, chives, butter, paprika, milk, cream, salt and pepper and purée. Return the soup to the saucepan and reheat. Sprinkle with chopped chives and paprika. Serve hot or cold.

Serves 6

Creamy Spinach Soup

1/4 cup (1/2 stick) butter or margarine
1   large onion, chopped
2   carrots, chopped
2   ribs celery with leaves, finely chopped
1/4 cup flour
3   cups water
2   cups diced potatoes
2   teaspoons salt
1   cup drained thawed frozen chopped
     spinach
3/4 cup heavy cream
     Shredded Swiss cheese or grated
     Parmesan cheese

Melt the butter in a large saucepan.
Add the onion, carrots and celery. Cook,
covered, over low heat until the vegetables
are tender, stirring occasionally. Stir in the
flour. Add the water, potatoes and salt.
Bring to a boil; reduce the heat to low and
simmer for 30 minutes. Add the spinach.
Simmer, uncovered, for 2 minutes. Add the
cream and cook until heated through.
Sprinkle with cheese.

Serves 6

Basil and Tomato Soup

3   tablespoons butter
1   large carrot, shredded
1   large onion, chopped
4   large ripe tomatoes, peeled, seeded
     and chopped
1/8 teaspoon pepper
3/4 cup sugar
1/4 cup lightly packed chopped fresh basil
1   (14-ounce) can chicken broth
1/4 cup lightly packed chopped fresh basil
     Salt to taste
     Chopped fresh parsley

Melt the butter in a 3-quart saucepan
over medium heat. Add the carrot and onion.
Cook until the onion is almost tender,
stirring frequently. Add the tomatoes,
pepper, sugar and 1/4 cup basil. Bring to a
boil, stirring constantly. Reduce the heat.
Simmer, covered, for 15 minutes. Purée
the tomato mixture in a blender or food
processor 1 portion at a time. Remove the
tomato mixture to the saucepan. Warm over
medium heat. Stir in the chicken broth,
1/4 cup basil and salt and cook until heated
through. Garnish with the parsley.

Serves 6

Between the Lakes

Sizzling Rice Soup

1	cup long-grain rice	1	whole boneless skinless chicken breast, sliced
1 1/2	cups water	1	teaspoon sesame oil
4	(14-ounce) cans chicken broth	1/2	cup dry sherry
1	cup chopped carrots	3	tablespoons soy sauce
1	cup sliced mushrooms	1	tablespoon rice wine vinegar
1	cup sliced bok choy stalks	1	teaspoon sesame oil
4	ounces cooked salad shrimp	1/2	cup chopped green onions
1/4	cup finely chopped fresh cilantro	1	cup chopped bok choy leaves
1/2	cup sliced water chestnuts	1	cup snow peas
1/2	cup sliced bamboo shoots		Vegetable oil for deep-frying

Rinse the rice. Bring the rice and 1 1/2 cups water to a boil in a saucepan. Reduce the heat, cover, and simmer for 30 minutes. Remove from the heat and cool. Spread the rice 1/4 inch thick on a baking sheet. Bake at 300 degrees for 50 to 55 minutes or until dry. Cut into squares and store in an airtight container.

Bring the broth, carrots, mushrooms, bok choy stalks, shrimp, cilantro, water chestnuts and bamboo shoots to a boil in a stockpot. Cover and simmer. Brown the chicken in 1 teaspoon sesame oil in a frying pan. Add the sherry and 1 tablespoon of the soy sauce. Cook until the liquid is reduced by 3/4 and the chicken is cooked through. Remove the chicken and add to the broth. Add the remaining 2 tablespoons soy sauce and the wine vinegar. Bring to a boil. Reduce the heat, cover, and simmer for 20 minutes. Add 1 teaspoon sesame oil, green onions, bok choy leaves and snow peas 5 minutes before serving and bring to a boil.

Heat the oil to 375 degrees in a kettle over medium high heat. Add the rice. Fry until slightly browned and remove with a slotted spoon. Place a rice square in each soup bowl and ladle the soup over the top.

Serves 10

Wild Rice Soup

1/2	cup wild rice
6	cups chicken stock
1/4	cup (1/2 stick) butter
2	ribs celery, diced
1	small onion, chopped
1	large carrot, diced
1/4	cup flour
1	cup finely diced ham
1/4	cup sherry
2 1/2	cups half-and-half
1/2	teaspoon salt
1/4	teaspoon white pepper
2	teaspoons granulated garlic, or less to taste

Rinse the rice thoroughly and place in a large saucepan. Add the chicken stock and bring to a boil. Reduce the heat, cover, and simmer until the grains just begin to pop. Strain the rice reserving the stock. Set aside. Melt the butter in a large saucepan. Add the celery, onion and carrot. Sauté the vegetables for 4 minutes. Stir in the flour and cook over medium heat for 2 minutes. Add the reserved stock and cook until slightly thickened, stirring constantly. Add the rice and ham. Simmer for 30 minutes or longer, stirring occasionally. Add the sherry, half-and-half, salt, white pepper and garlic. Simmer for 30 minutes.

Note: This soup freezes well.

Serves about 10

Between the Lakes

Main Courses

Pork Medallions with
Michigan Apple and
Cherry Chutney
Grilled Spareribs with
Cherry Cola Glaze
Candied Apple Pork Chops
Pork Chops with Maple Glaze
Italian Pork Chops
Pork Chops with Vermouth
Maple Baked Ham and
Sweet Potatoes
Italian Sausage Gravy
Beef Tenderloin
Perfect Prime Rib
Short Ribs
Filets Mignons with
Mushroom and Leek Sauce
Gorgonzola Sauce
Beef Satay
Peanut Sauce
Flank Steak
Steak Marinade for Flank Steak
Hot Beef Sandwiches Au Jus
Goulash
Beef Burgundy
Veal Scaloppine with Wine
Marinated Roast Leg of Lamb
Lamb Chops with Lemon and Dill
Apple Mountain's Chicken Kathleen
Balsamic Marinated Chicken
Lemon Rosemary Chicken
Chicken and Bacon

Chicken Bake with
Swiss Cheese and Ham
The Chef's Table Crusty
Mustard Chicken
Elegant Chicken and Pasta
Chicken and Chile Chimichangas
Chicken and Rice
Fish Florentine
Creole Pasta
Baked Lemon Pepper Salmon
with Capers
Creamy Salmon Pasta
Grilled Salmon Teriyaki
Michigan Trout with Mushrooms
Fish a la Greque
Asiago-Encrusted Walleye
Baked Stuffed Whitefish
Mussels in Wine
Baked Sea Scallops
Broiled Curried Sea Scallops
Low Country Shrimp and
Sausage Roast
Saginaw Spaghetti
Scrumptious Spinach Lasagna
Pasta Bows with
Roasted Pepper Sauce
Roasted Pheasant
Pheasant and Smoked
Sausage Gumbo
Pheasant and Mushrooms
Venison Stroganoff
Lake Superior Cooking

Main Courses

Pork Medallions with Michigan Apple and Cherry Chutney

2	pounds pork tenderloin	2	to 3 tablespoons
1	cup flour		canola oil
1	teaspoon salt		Apple and Cherry Chutney
1/2	teaspoon pepper		(see below)

Trim the fat from the pork. Slice 1/2 inch thick. Place the pork between 2 sheets of plastic wrap and pound 1/4 inch thick. Dust the pork with flour, salt and pepper. Heat the oil in a large skillet over medium-high heat. Add the pork and sauté on both sides until browned and cooked through. Serve the pork with Apple and Cherry Chutney.

Serves 4 to 6

Apple and Cherry Chutney

1	tablespoon butter	1/4	cup apple cider vinegar
1/4	onion, chopped		Pinch of nutmeg
1	apple, peeled and diced		Pinch of allspice
1/3	cup dried cherries		Salt and pepper to taste
1/3	cup packed brown sugar		

Melt the butter in a medium skillet over medium heat. Add the onion and sauté until tender. Add the apple, cherries, brown sugar, vinegar, nutmeg and allspice. Bring the chutney to a simmer. Simmer the chutney until the liquid is reduced and has a sauce consistency, stirring occasionally. Add the salt and pepper.

Grilled Spareribs with Cherry Cola Glaze

4	(12-ounce) cans cherry cola
2	cups cherry jam or preserves
2/3	cup Dijon mustard with horseradish
3	tablespoons soy sauce
2	tablespoons malt vinegar or apple cider vinegar
1	tablespoon hot pepper sauce
7 1/4	to 7 1/2 pounds well-trimmed pork spareribs
	Salt and pepper to taste

Pour the cherry cola into a bowl. Let stand at room temperature for 4 hours or until no longer effervescent. Boil the cola in a large heavy saucepan over medium-high heat for 45 minutes or until reduced to 1 1/2 cups. Stir in the jam, mustard, soy sauce, vinegar and hot pepper sauce. Reduce the heat to medium. Simmer for 35 minutes or until reduced to 2 1/2 cups, stirring occasionally. Pour into a large bowl. (You may prepare up to 1 week ahead and store, covered, in the refrigerator. Bring to room temperature before using.)

Position the oven racks in the top and bottom thirds of the oven. Sprinkle the ribs with salt and pepper. Wrap each rib rack tightly in foil to enclose completely. Divide the foil packets between 2 shallow baking pans. Bake at 325 degrees for 2 hours or until the ribs are tender and cooked through, switching the positions of the baking pans halfway through baking. Cool the ribs slightly. Pour off any liquid from the packets. (You may prepare up to 1 day ahead. Keep covered in foil and refrigerate. Let stand at room temperature for 1 hour before continuing.)

Remove the rib racks from the foil packets and cut each rib rack between the bones into individual ribs. Reserve 1 cup of the glaze. Coat the ribs with the remaining glaze. Place on a grill rack. Grill over medium-low heat for 5 minutes or until brown and glazed, turning to prevent burning. Serve the ribs with the reserved glaze.

Serves 6

Between the Lakes

Candied Apple Pork Chops

Chef Feinauer, Heatherfield's

2	(10-ounce) center cut bone-in pork chops	1/2	cup packed brown sugar
1/4	large Spanish onion, julienned	1/2	teaspoon cinnamon
2	Red Delicious apples, cored and sliced	1/4	cup Apple Barrel schnapps

Sear the pork chops in a skillet for 5 minutes on each side. Remove the pork chops to a platter and keep warm. Add the onion to the skillet. Sauté until the onion is translucent. Add the apples. Sauté for 2 minutes. Stir in the brown sugar and cinnamon. Add the schnapps carefully since it may flame. Return the pork chops to the skillet. Cook until the pork chops register 160 degrees on a meat thermometer.

Serves 2

Pork Chops with Maple Glaze

2	tablespoons shortening	1 1/2	teaspoons salt
6	pork chops	1/2	teaspoon pepper
1/4	cup chopped onion	1/2	teaspoon chili powder
1	tablespoon vinegar	1/4	cup maple syrup
1	tablespoon Worcestershire sauce	1/4	cup water

Melt the shortening in a large heavy ovenproof skillet. Add the pork and brown on both sides. Combine the onion, vinegar, Worcestershire sauce, salt, pepper, chili powder, maple syrup and water in a bowl and mix well. Pour over the pork. Bake, covered, at 375 degrees for 45 minutes, basting often. Uncover the pork and bake for 15 minutes longer.

Serves 6

APPLES

Apple volume is greater than that of all the other Michigan fruits combined. Apples are an excellent source of nutrition. Just one apple provides as much dietary fiber as a serving of bran cereal. Keeping apples crisp means keeping them cold. All apples should be refrigerated to prevent quick ripening. Dipping peeled apples in lemon juice or salt water prevents the flesh from darkening.

Italian Pork Chops

1/4   cup flour
      Salt and pepper to taste
4   center-cut pork chops
3   tablespoons extra-virgin olive oil
3/4   cup white wine
6   kalamata olives, pitted and chopped
6   cured green olives, pitted and chopped
1/4   cup white wine

Place the flour, salt and pepper in a non-recycled paper bag. Add the pork chops and shake to coat. Heat the oil in a large skillet over medium-high heat just until it begins to smoke. Add the pork. Reduce the heat to medium and brown the pork on both sides. Add 3/4 cup white wine and cook until most of the wine evaporates. Remove the pork to a plate and keep warm. Add the kalamata olives, green olives and 1/4 cup wine. Scrape up any browned bits in the skillet. Pour the olive sauce over the pork and serve immediately.

Serves 4

Pork Chops with Vermouth

4   pork chops
      Sage to taste
      Paprika to taste
2   tablespoons vegetable oil
1   (10-ounce) can consommé
1/2   cup dry vermouth

Rub the pork chops with sage and paprika. Heat the oil in a large skillet over medium-high heat just until it begins to smoke. Add the pork. Reduce the heat to medium and brown the pork on both sides. Add the consommé. Cook, covered, over medium heat for 45 minutes. Add the dry vermouth and cook for 15 minutes longer.

Serves 4

Between the Lakes

Maple Baked Ham and Sweet Potatoes

1 1/2 precooked ham steaks
    (about 2 pounds)
8   whole cloves
6   sweet potatoes, peeled
1   cup maple syrup
1/4   cup boiling water

Trim and reserve the fat from the ham. Place the ham in a heavy baking pan. Stud the fat with cloves and arrange it around the ham. Combine the sweet potatoes with enough water to cover in a saucepan. Bring to a boil. Boil for 10 minutes; drain. Cut the sweet potatoes lengthwise into thick slices. Place the sweet potatoes around the ham. Blend the maple syrup and boiling water in a bowl. Pour over the ham and sweet potatoes. Cover the dish. Bake at 400 degrees for 1 hour or until the sweet potatoes are tender, basting often with the pan juices. Discard the fat. Cut the ham into serving-size pieces. Serve the ham and sweet potatoes with the pan juices.

Serves 6

Italian Sausage Gravy

1   pound bulk pork sausage
1   large onion, chopped
1   green bell pepper, finely chopped
1   (15-ounce) can tomato purée
2   (6-ounce) cans tomato paste
1 1/2   cups water
1   (28-ounce) can peeled whole tomatoes
2   garlic cloves, minced
1/4   teaspoon oregano
1/2   teaspoon freshly ground pepper
    Pinch of basil
1 1/2   teaspoons salt
1   tablespoon sugar, or more to taste
    Cooked pasta

Brown the sausage in a large skillet, stirring until crumbly. Add the onion and bell pepper and brown; drain. Add the tomato purée, tomato paste, water, whole tomatoes, garlic, oregano, pepper, basil, salt and sugar and mix well. Bring to a boil. Reduce the heat to low. Simmer, covered, for 2 to 3 hours, stirring every 15 minutes. Adjust the sugar. Serve over pasta.

Serves 4 to 6

Beef Tenderloin

1   (4- to 5-pound) beef tenderloin
5   tablespoons softened butter
1/2 cup chopped green onions
1   pound fresh mushrooms, sliced
1/4 cup soy sauce
1   tablespoon Dijon mustard

Spread the tenderloin with 2 tablespoons butter. Place the tenderloin on a rack in a roasting pan. Roast at 400 degrees for 20 minutes. Melt the remaining butter in a large skillet. Add the green onions and sauté until tender. Add the mushrooms and sauté. Stir in the soy sauce and mustard. Cook until the mushrooms are tender. Add to the tenderloin and roast for 20 to 25 minutes longer.

Serves 8 to 10

Perfect Prime Rib

Prime rib (any size)

Place the prime rib on a rack in a roasting pan. Roast at 370 degrees for 1 hour. Turn off the heat. Do not open the oven door. Let stand in the oven for up to 2 hours. Roast at 300 degrees for 45 minutes longer for rare; 50 minutes for medium-rare and 55 minutes for medium. Remove from the oven. Let stand for 10 minutes before carving.

Serves a variable amount

Short Ribs

4   pounds short ribs
2   onions, sliced
1   (15-ounce) can tomato sauce
1   cup water
1/4 cup packed light brown sugar
1/4 cup vinegar
1   teaspoon dry mustard
1   teaspoon salt
1   teaspoon Worcestershire sauce

Place the short ribs in a Dutch oven and brown on all sides. Add the onions, tomato sauce, water, brown sugar, vinegar, dry mustard, salt and Worcestershire sauce. Roast at 300 degrees for 2 to 2 1/2 hours.

Serves 4

Between the Lakes

Filets Mignons with Mushroom and Leek Sauce

1   tablespoon olive oil
1   tablespoon butter
4   (6-ounce) filets mignons
1   tablespoon olive oil
1   leek, white part only, julienned
1   cup sliced mushrooms (use a variety)
4   to 5 tablespoons beef stock
4   to 5 dashes of Worcestershire sauce
4   to 5 tablespoons red wine
     Salt and pepper to taste
2   to 3 tablespoons butter

Combine 1 tablespoon olive oil and 1 tablespoon butter in an ovenproof sauté pan over high heat. Add the filets mignons and brown for 2 minutes on each side. Roast the filets mignons at 350 degrees for 10 minutes. Remove to a plate and keep warm. Drain the fat from the pan. Add 1 tablespoon olive oil. Add the leek and sauté for 1 to 2 minutes. Add the mushrooms and sauté for 2 to 3 minutes longer. Add the beef stock, Worcestershire sauce and red wine. Cook over medium-high heat to reduce by 1/2. Add the salt and pepper. Just before serving swirl in the butter. Serve the mushroom and leek sauce over the filets mignons.

Serves 4

Gorgonzola Sauce

4   cups heavy cream
3   to 4 ounces firm Gorgonzola cheese, crumbled
3   tablespoons freshly grated Parmesan cheese
3/4 teaspoon kosher salt
3/4 teaspoon freshly ground pepper
3   tablespoons minced fresh parsley

Pour the cream into a medium saucepan. Bring to a boil over medium-high heat. Boil until the cream is as thick as a white sauce, stirring occasionally. Remove from the heat. Whisk in the Gorgonzola cheese, Parmesan cheese, kosher salt, pepper and parsley. Whisk rapidly until the cheeses melt. Serve the Gorgonzola Sauce warm over steak or roast beef.

Note: If you must reheat the sauce, place the saucepan over low heat until the cheese melts. Then whisk vigorously until the sauce comes together.

Makes 3 cups

Beef Satay

1/3   cup canola oil
1/3   cup packed fresh cilantro with stems
1/4   cup lime juice
1/4   cup tamari sauce
1   (1-inch) piece gingerroot, peeled
8   garlic cloves, crushed and peeled
1 1/2 tablespoons sugar
1   tablespoon cumin
1   small dry red chile, or 1 tablespoon
      red pepper flakes
8   ounces flank steak, or boneless and
      skinless chicken breasts, cut into
      strips 2 inches long and 1/2 inch wide
      Peanut Sauce (at right)

Place the canola oil, cilantro, lime juice, tamari sauce, gingerroot, garlic, sugar, cumin and chile in a blender and process until the cilantro and chile are finely chopped. Pour the cilantro mixture into a nonreactive bowl. Add the beef strips and marinate in the refrigerator for one hour. Soak wooden skewers in water. Thread the beef strips lengthwise on the skewers. Place on a grill rack. Grill over medium-hot coals for 2 to 3 minutes per side or to the desired degree of doneness. Serve with the Peanut Sauce.

Serves 4

Peanut Sauce

1   (14-ounce) can unsweetened
      coconut milk
1 1/3 cups peanut butter
1/2   cup heavy cream
2   tablespoons soy sauce
      Juice of 1 lime
4   garlic cloves
1   (2-inch) piece gingerroot, peeled and
      coarsely chopped
1/4   cup plus 1 tablespoon sugar
1   teaspoon crushed red pepper flakes
1/2   teaspoon cayenne pepper
1/2   teaspoon coriander
1/2   teaspoon cumin

Purée the coconut milk, peanut butter, heavy cream, soy sauce, lime juice, garlic, gingerroot, sugar, red pepper flakes, cayenne pepper, coriander and cumin in a blender or food processor.

Serves 4

Between the Lakes

Flank Steak

1	(1½-pound) flank steak	3	tablespoons soy sauce
4	to 6 scallions, minced, or 2 tablespoons dried minced onion	3	tablespoons olive oil
		1	teaspoon thyme
			Pepper to taste
			Juice of ½ lemon

Score the steak on both sides. Combine the scallions, soy sauce, olive oil, thyme, pepper and lemon juice in a shallow non-reactive bowl. Add the steak and marinate in the refrigerator for 30 minutes. Place the steak on a rack in a broiler pan. Broil 2 inches from the heat source for 5 minutes. Turn over and broil for 4 minutes longer for medium-rare. Slice the steak diagonally across grain.

Serves 4 to 6

Steak Marinade for Flank Steak

¼	cup ketchup	1	tablespoon Worcestershire sauce
⅓	cup wine vinegar		
¼	teaspoon garlic powder	1	teaspoon salt
2	tablespoons vegetable oil	¼	teaspoon pepper
2	tablespoons soy sauce	1	(1½-pound) flank steak

Combine the ketchup, vinegar, garlic powder, oil, soy sauce, Worcestershire sauce, salt and pepper in a sealable plastic bag. Add the steak. Marinate in the refrigerator for at least 3 hours. Remove from the marinade. Grill the steak over medium-hot coals to the desired degree of doneness.

Serves 4 to 6

Hot Beef Sandwiches Au Jus

1   (4- to 5-pound) beef rump roast
1   envelope onion soup mix
2   teaspoons sugar
1   teaspoon oregano
2   (10-ounce) cans condensed beef broth
1   (12-ounce) can beer
2   garlic cloves, minced
16 onion buns

Place the beef in a 3½ to 4-quart slow cooker. Combine the onion soup mix, sugar, oregano, broth, beer and garlic in a large bowl and mix well. Pour over the roast. Cook on Low for 8 to 10 hours. Slice or shred the beef and serve in the buns. Skim the fat from the juices. Serve the sandwiches with the beef juices for dipping.

Makes 16 sandwiches

Goulash

1   pound ground beef
1   garlic clove, minced
1   small onion, finely chopped
1   (14-ounce) can diced tomatoes
1   (8-ounce) can tomato sauce
2   teaspoons basil
1   tablespoon sugar
    Salt and pepper to taste
8   ounces noodles, cooked
1   cup (4 ounces) shredded sharp Cheddar cheese
    Chopped parsley to taste

Brown the ground beef with garlic and onion in a skillet, stirring until crumbly; drain. Add the tomatoes, tomato sauce, basil, sugar, salt and pepper. Stir in the noodles. Layer the beef mixture and cheese ½ at a time in a baking dish, ending with the cheese. Bake at 350 degrees for 45 minutes. Sprinkle with parsley before serving.

Serves 4

Beef Burgundy

6	slices bacon
1	pound lean beef chuck, 1/2 inch thick, cut into cubes
1/2	cup flour
1	teaspoon salt
1	cup burgundy
2	tablespoons chopped fresh parsley
1/2	garlic clove
1/2	teaspoon thyme
1	(10-ounce) can condensed beef broth
1	tablespoon tomato paste
6	potatoes, peeled and halved
3	or 4 carrots, diced
1	(15-ounce) jar small onions, drained
8	ounces fresh mushrooms
1	tablespoon butter

Place the bacon in a skillet and cook over medium-high heat until the bacon is crisp-cooked. Remove the bacon with a slotted spoon and drain on paper towels. Reserve the bacon drippings in the skillet. Crumble the bacon and set aside. Place the beef cubes a few at a time in a non-recycled paper bag with the flour and salt. Shake to coat. Brown the beef on all sides in the bacon drippings. Remove the beef to a 2- to 3-quart baking dish. Pour the burgundy into a blender. Add the parsley, garlic, thyme and beef broth and purée. Stir in the tomato paste. Pour the burgundy mixture over the beef. Cover the dish. Bake at 350 degrees for 1 hour. Stir in the potatoes, carrots and onions. Cover and bake for 1 hour longer. Sauté the mushrooms in the butter in a skillet. Stir the sautéed mushrooms and bacon into the beef mixture.

Note: If desired, omit the potatoes and serve the Beef Burgundy over buttered noodles.

Serves 4 or 5

Veal Scaloppine with Wine

2	pounds thinly sliced, trimmed veal cutlets or boneless skinless chicken breasts, pounded thin		1	tablespoon olive oil
	Salt and pepper to taste		1/4	cup (1/2 stick) butter
	Garlic salt to taste		11/2	cups sliced mushrooms
1/2	cup (2 ounces) grated Parmesan cheese		1/2	cup chopped scallions
3	tablespoons flour		1	cup diced green bell pepper
1/4	cup (1/2 stick) butter		1	cup dry white wine
			1/2	cup dry sherry
			4	beef bouillon cubes
				Parsley for garnish

Cut the veal into individual serving pieces. Season with the salt, pepper and garlic salt. Combine the Parmesan cheese and flour on a plate. Dredge the veal in the Parmesan cheese mixture. Heat 1/4 cup butter and the olive oil in a large skillet. Add the veal a few pieces at a time and sauté until golden on both sides. Remove and keep warm. Melt 1/4 cup butter in a second skillet. Add the mushrooms, scallions and bell pepper and sauté until tender. Remove from the heat. Place the veal and vegetables in a Dutch oven. Mix the wine, sherry and bouillon cubes in a bowl, stirring to dissolve the bouillon cubes. Pour the wine mixture over the veal. Simmer, covered, for 15 minutes. Remove the veal to a serving plate and garnish with parsley. Serve with cooked green noodles tossed with sour cream, butter and grated Parmesan cheese.

Serves 8

Marinated Roast Leg of Lamb

1   leg of lamb
1/2   cup olive oil
2   teaspoons salt
1   teaspoon pepper
      Juice of 2 lemons
1   garlic clove
1   onion, chopped
      Assorted herbs including thyme,
      parsley, oregano and bay leaf
2   cups red or white wine

Place the lamb in a non-reactive container. Combine the olive oil, salt, pepper, lemon juice, garlic, onion, herbs and wine in a bowl and mix well. Pour the wine mixture over the lamb. Marinate, covered, in the refrigerator for 24 hours, turning the lamb several times. Place the lamb on a rack in a roasting pan. Roast at 300 degrees until a meat thermometer registers 165 degrees for medium doneness, basting occasionally if the lamb does not have a layer of fat. For medium well-done lamb allow 22 to 26 minutes per pound. Serve the lamb with pan juices.

Serves 8 to 10

Lamb Chops with Lemon and Dill

1/3   cup fresh lemon juice
1/3   cup snipped fresh dill weed, or
      3 tablespoons dried dill weed
2   tablespoons Dijon mustard
1   teaspoon salt
1/3   cup vegetable oil
12   to 18 small lamb chops, cut 1 inch to
      1 1/4 inches thick

Combine the lemon juice, dill weed, mustard, salt and oil in a large glass dish and mix well. Add the lamb chops turning to coat both sides. Cover with plastic wrap. Marinate in the refrigerator for 8 to 12 hours, turning the lamb chops several times. Remove the lamb chops and drain the marinade. Place on a grill rack or on a rack in a broiler pan. Grill or broil the lamb for 4 minutes on the first side and for 3 minutes on the second side for medium doneness.

Serves 4 to 6

Apple Mountain's Chicken Kathleen

1	cup half-and-half	2	tablespoons butter
1	tablespoon minced shallot		Splash of white wine
1	teaspoon Worcestershire sauce	1	Maggi cube
			Splash of olive oil
1/4	ounce garlic	1/4	cup dried bread crumbs
5	ounces Boursin cheese	1	cup (4 ounces) shredded mozzarella cheese
1/3	cup white wine		
4	ounces roux	2	eggs, beaten
	Salt and pepper to taste	6	large boneless skinless chicken breasts
4	ounces lump crab meat		
3	ounces snow crab meat	1	egg, beaten
2	ounces minced cooked shrimp	1	tablespoon water
		1/4	cup flour
3	tablespoons each minced bell pepper, parsley, celery and onion	1	cup coarse Oriental bread crumbs
			Butter for sautéing

Cook the half-and-half in a saucepan until reduced by 1/3. Sauté the shallot in a large nonstick skillet until transparent. Add the reduced half-and-half and simmer briefly. Stir in the Worcestershire sauce and next 3 ingredients. Add the roux, salt and pepper. Cook until the desired consistency, stirring constantly. Keep warm or chill to 40 degrees. Sauté the crab meat and next 5 ingredients in 2 tablespoons butter in a skillet until soft. Add a splash of wine and the next 5 ingredients and stir gently. Chill to 40 degrees or below. Pound the chicken between plastic wrap until 1/4 inch thick. Place 1 tablespoon of the seafood filling on the short width end of each chicken breast and roll up. Secure with wooden picks. Whisk 1 egg and water in a bowl. Mix the flour, salt and pepper together. Coat each roll-up with the egg mixture; dredge in the flour mixture. Freeze for 30 to 40 minutes. Coat with the remaining egg mixture. Roll in the bread crumbs. Sauté in butter in a skillet until brown. Place on a baking sheet. Bake at 325 degrees for 20 minutes or until cooked through. Cut into slices and serve with the sauce.

Serves 6

Between the Lakes

Balsamic Marinated Chicken

1/4   cup balsamic vinegar
1/4   cup honey
1/4   cup olive oil
2   tablespoons chopped fresh rosemary
1   teaspoon salt
3   pounds chicken (combination of
      breasts, thighs and drumsticks)

Combine the vinegar, honey, olive oil, rosemary and salt in a large sealable plastic bag. Add the chicken and seal the bag. Marinate in the refrigerator for 2 hours, turning occasionally. Place the chicken in a lightly greased 9×13-inch baking dish. Pour the marinade over the chicken. Bake at 375 degrees for 45 minutes or until the chicken is cooked through, basting often with pan drippings.

Serves 4

Lemon Rosemary Chicken

1/2   cup olive oil
1/4   cup fresh lemon juice
1   garlic clove, minced
2   tablespoons chopped fresh rosemary,
      or 2 teaspoons dried rosemary
2   tablespoons chopped green onions
2   teaspoons grated lemon zest
1/2   teaspoon salt
      Freshly ground pepper to taste
4   boneless skinless chicken breasts

Whisk the olive oil, lemon juice, garlic, rosemary, green onions, lemon zest, salt and pepper together in a bowl. Place the chicken in a non-reactive bowl and pour on the marinade. Marinate, covered, in the refrigerator for 4 to 5 hours. Remove the chicken and reserve the marinade. Place the marinade in a saucepan and boil for 2 to 3 minutes, stirring constantly. Grill or broil the chicken over indirect high heat for 20 minutes or until the juices run clear, basting frequently with the marinade. Serve the cooked marinade along with the chicken.

Serves 4

Chicken and Bacon

12 slices bacon, crisp-cooked
6   whole chicken breasts, cut into
    halves, or 12 chicken tenders
12 slices dried beef
12 ounces mushrooms, sliced
1   tablespoon butter
2   (10-ounce) cans cream of chicken
    soup
2   cups sour cream
1   (3-ounce) package cream cheese,
    softened
1   cup buttered bread crumbs

Place the bacon in the bottom of a
9×12-inch baking dish. Arrange the chicken
breasts over the bacon. Rinse the dried
beef to remove some of the salt. Place the
dried beef over the chicken. Sauté the
mushrooms in the butter in a skillet to
remove some of the liquid. Spoon the
mushrooms over the dried beef. Mix the
chicken soup, sour cream and cream
cheese together in a bowl. Spoon over the
mushrooms. Cover the baking dish with
foil. Bake at 325 degrees for 1½ hours.
Remove the foil, sprinkle with the bread
crumbs and bake for 15 minutes longer.

Serves 12

Chicken Bake with Swiss Cheese and Ham

2   tablespoons butter or margarine
1/2 cup chopped onion
3   tablespoons flour
1/2 teaspoon salt
1/4 teaspoon pepper
1   (3-ounce) can sliced mushrooms
1   cup light cream
2   tablespoons dry sherry
2   cups cubed cooked chicken
1   cup cubed cooked ham
1   (5-ounce) can sliced water chestnuts,
     drained
1/2 cup (2 ounces) shredded Swiss cheese
1½   cups bread crumbs
3   tablespoons melted butter or
     margarine

Melt 2 tablespoons butter in a large
saucepan. Add the onion and cook until
tender, but not brown. Stir in the flour, salt
and pepper. Add the mushrooms, cream
and sherry. Cook until thickened, stirring
constantly. Add the chicken, ham and water
chestnuts. Pour the chicken mixture into
a 1½-quart baking dish. Sprinkle with the
cheese. Combine the bread crumbs and
3 tablespoons butter in a bowl. Spread the
bread crumbs over the cheese. Bake at
400 degrees for 25 minutes or until the
bread crumbs are lightly browned.

Serves 4 to 6

Between the Lakes

The Chef's Table Crusty Mustard Chicken

4   boneless skinless chicken breasts
       Flour for dusting
1   cup heavy cream
2   tablespoons Dijon mustard
       Panko (Japanese bread crumbs)
       Clarified butter (optional)
2   cups cream
2   teaspoons chopped fresh basil
       Salt and pepper to taste

Dust the chicken with flour. Combine the heavy cream and mustard in a bowl. Coat the chicken with the mustard mixture. Place the panko on a plate. Roll the chicken in panko to coat. Heat the clarified butter in a large skillet. Add the chicken and sauté until golden brown and cooked through. Remove the chicken and keep warm.

Place the cream in a saucepan and bring to a boil. Cook over medium heat until reduced by 1/2. Stir in the basil, salt and pepper. Drizzle the chicken with the basil-cream sauce.

Variation: Use 1 pound medium shrimp, peeled and deveined.

Serves 4

Elegant Chicken and Pasta

1/4   cup (1/2 stick) butter
1   envelope Italian salad dressing mix
1/2   cup white wine
1   (10-ounce) can cream of mushroom
       soup
4   ounces cream cheese with chives,
       softened
6   boneless skinless chicken breasts, cut
       into pieces
1   pound angel hair pasta
       Salt to taste

Melt the butter in a large saucepan over low heat. Stir in the dressing mix. Stir in the wine and mushroom soup. Add the cream cheese and mix well. Cook until heated through, but do not boil. Arrange the chicken in a single layer in a 9×13-inch baking dish. Pour the sauce over the chicken. Bake at 325 degrees for 1 hour. Cook the pasta in boiling salted water in a large saucepan for 5 minutes or until al dente; drain. Serve the chicken and sauce over the pasta.

Serves 6 to 8

Chicken and Chile Chimichangas

2	(5-ounce) boneless skinless chicken breasts
1/2	teaspoon cumin or taco seasoning mix
1	cup (4 ounces) shredded reduced-fat Monterey Jack or mozzarella cheese
1	(4-ounce) can diced mild green chiles
6	(7-inch) flour tortillas
	Green Onion and Cilantro Sauce (see below)

Bring 4 cups of water to a boil in a large saucepan over high heat. Add the chicken, cover and remove from heat. Let stand for 15 minutes or until the chicken is no longer pink in the center. Drain and let cool slightly. Tear the chicken into small pieces. Place the chicken in a bowl and sprinkle with cumin. Add the cheese and chiles and mix well. Spoon about 1/2 cup chicken mixture down the center of each tortilla. Fold the sides to overlap at the center; secure with wooden picks. Brush each chimichanga lightly with water, coating all around. Place the chimichangas 1 inch apart on a baking sheet. Bake at 400 degrees for 12 to 15 minutes or until the tortillas are crisp and just barely golden. Serve with shredded romaine lettuce, sliced tomatoes and Green Onion and Cilantro Sauce.

Serves 6

Green Onion and Cilantro Sauce

1/4	cup plain fat-free yogurt
1/4	cup low-fat sour cream
1/3	cup chopped green onions
1/3	cup lightly packed fresh cilantro

Purée the yogurt, sour cream, green onions and cilantro in a blender or food processor.

Note: If desired use 1/2 cup fat-free yogurt, red onion and parsley.

Chicken and Rice

2 to 3 pounds boneless skinless chicken breasts
1 cup water
1 cup dry sherry
1 1/2 teaspoons salt
1/2 teaspoon curry powder
2 (6-ounce) packages flavored wild rice mix
1/4 cup (1/2 stick) margarine
1/2 cup diced celery
1 pound fresh mushrooms, sliced
1 onion, chopped
1 cup mushroom soup
1 cup sour cream

Place the chicken breasts in a large saucepan. Add the water, sherry, salt and curry powder. Cook for 15 to 20 minutes. Cook the rice according to the package directions. Set aside. Melt the margarine in a large skillet. Add the celery, mushrooms and onion and sauté. Cut the chicken into bite-size pieces. Mix the chicken, rice, sautéed vegetables, soup and sour cream together in a mixing bowl. Spoon into a 9x13-inch baking dish. Bake at 350 degrees for 1 hour or longer.

Serves 6

Fish Florentine

1/2 bunch fresh spinach or Swiss chard
1 tablespoon margarine
   Salt and pepper to taste
1/4 cup (1 ounce) grated Parmesan cheese
4 orange roughy, tilapia or flounder fillets
   Juice of 1 lemon or lime
1 tablespoon margarine
1/2 to 1 cup bread crumbs
1 tablespoon margarine

Rinse and dry the spinach. Steam until tender. Place the spinach in a buttered baking dish. Dot with 1 tablespoon margarine. Add the salt and pepper and sprinkle with 1/3 of the cheese. Arrange the orange roughy over the cheese. Squeeze lemon juice on the fish. Dot with 1 tablespoon margarine. Sprinkle with 1/2 the remaining cheese and bread crumbs. Dot with 1 tablespoon margarine and sprinkle with the remaining cheese. Bake at 350 degrees for 20 minutes.

Serves 4

Creole Pasta

1/2	cup boned, skinned and julienned chicken breast
1	teaspoon Creole seasoning
1	tablespoon olive oil
2	ounces chopped andouille sausage or chorizo
8	ounces peeled and deveined medium shrimp
1 1/2	teaspoons Creole seasoning
1/4	cup chopped green onions
1	tablespoon minced garlic
1 1/2	cups heavy cream
1/4	teaspoon Worcestershire sauce
1/4	teaspoon hot red pepper sauce
1/2	teaspoon salt
1/4	cup coarsely grated Parmesan cheese
8	ounces fettuccine or rotini
1/4	cup coarsely grated Parmesan cheese

Toss the chicken strips with 1 teaspoon Creole seasoning in a bowl. Heat the olive oil in a large skillet over high heat. Add the chicken strips and sauté for 1 minute, shaking the skillet occasionally. Add the sausage and cook for 1 minute, shaking the skillet and stirring. Add the shrimp and 1 1/2 teaspoons Creole seasoning. Sauté for 1 minute. Stir in the green onions, garlic and cream and cook for 2 minutes. Stir in the Worcestershire sauce, hot red pepper sauce, salt and 1/4 cup cheese and simmer for 3 minutes. Cook the pasta using the package directions until al dente; drain. Add the pasta to the chicken mixture. Cook for 1 minute, stirring constantly. Remove from the heat. Sprinkle each serving with 1 tablespoon cheese.

Serves 4

Baked Lemon Pepper Salmon with Capers

1/2   cup chopped shallots
1/4   cup drained capers
1   tablespoon fresh dill weed, or
      1 teaspoon dried dill weed
1   (1¼-pound) skinless center-cut
      salmon fillet
1   tablespoon lemon pepper
      Lemon wedges

Combine the shallots, capers and dill weed in a small bowl. Place the salmon on a large sheet of foil sprayed with nonstick baking spray. Sprinkle with lemon pepper. Spread the shallot mixture over the salmon. Fold up the foil edges to enclose salmon and seal. Place the salmon on a baking sheet. Bake at 425 degrees for 28 to 30 minutes or until the salmon is opaque in the center. Remove the salmon to a platter. Spoon the cooking juices over the salmon and garnish with lemon wedges.

Serves 4

Creamy Salmon Pasta

8   ounces shell pasta (conchiglie)
1/2   cup frozen peas
4   Roma tomatoes
1½   cups fat-free milk
3   tablespoons leek soup mix
1   tablespoon margarine
1/2   cup (2 ounces) grated Parmesan
      cheese
1   teaspoon Worcestershire sauce
1/4   teaspoon dill weed
1   tablespoon flour
1   (7-ounce) package flaked salmon
      Salt and pepper to taste

Cook the pasta using the package directions until al dente; drain. Place the peas in a colander and hold under running water for 30 seconds. Drain and set aside. Core the tomatoes and cut into bite-size pieces; set aside. Combine the milk and soup mix in a saucepan. Cook over low heat, whisking constantly to remove any lumps. Cut the margarine into small pieces and add to the milk mixture. Add the cheese, Worcestershire sauce and dill weed. Cook over high heat until the margarine and cheese melt. Sprinkle in the flour and reduce the heat to low. Cook until the sauce has the consistency of pudding, stirring constantly. Add the salmon, peas and tomatoes. Sprinkle with salt and pepper. Remove the pasta to a plate and top with the salmon.

Serves 4

Grilled Salmon Teriyaki

1/3 cup orange juice
1/3 cup soy sauce
1/4 cup dry white wine
2 tablespoons vegetable oil
1 teaspoon ground ginger, or 1
    tablespoon fresh gingerroot, minced
1 teaspoon dry mustard
1 teaspoon lemon juice
    Pinch of sugar
1 garlic clove, minced
1/2 teaspoon pepper
16 to 20 ounces salmon fillet, skinned

Combine the orange juice, soy sauce, wine, oil, ginger, dry mustard, lemon juice, sugar, garlic and pepper in a plastic bag. Add the salmon. Marinate in the refrigerator for 30 minutes, turning once. Remove the salmon and reserve the marinade. Grill the salmon in a grill basket for 10 to 15 minutes or until the fish flakes easily, turning once. Place the marinade in a saucepan and boil for 6 to 8 minutes or until reduced by half. Pour the cooked marinade over the salmon.

Serves 4

Michigan Trout with Mushrooms

4 cleaned whole brook or brown trout
    Flour for dusting
    Salt and pepper to taste
2 tablespoons butter
2 tablespoons olive oil
2 tablespoons butter
8 ounces mushrooms, sliced
1 teaspoon lemon juice
1 tablespoon butter
3/4 cup thinly sliced green onions
1 tablespoon butter
1/2 cup fresh bread crumbs from
    French bread

Rinse the trout and pat dry. Dust with the flour, salt and pepper. Heat 2 tablespoons butter and the olive oil in a large skillet. Add the trout. Sauté for 4 to 5 minutes to brown. Set aside. Melt 2 tablespoons butter in a large skillet. Add the mushrooms and sauté. Sprinkle with the lemon juice; set aside. Melt 1 tablespoon butter in a skillet. Add the green onions and cook for 1 minute. Remove to a bowl. Melt 1 tablespoon butter in a skillet. Add the bread crumbs and brown. Spread the mushrooms on an ovenproof platter. Arrange the trout over the mushrooms. Spread on the bread crumbs and green onions. Bake at 425 degrees for 10 minutes.

Serves 4

Between the Lakes

Fish a la Greque

4	ounces feta or seasoned feta cheese, crumbled	2	small plum tomatoes, seeded, chopped and drained
1/4	cup plain low-fat yogurt		
1/4	cup finely chopped onion	4	(6-ounce) walleye pike fillets, 1/2 inch thick
3	tablespoons drained capers		
		1	lemon, halved

Combine the cheese, yogurt, onion, capers and tomatoes in a bowl and mix well. Place the fish fillets on a baking sheet lined with foil sprayed with nonstick baking spray. Spread the cheese mixture on the fish. Squeeze the lemon on the fish. Bake at 400 degrees for 10 to 20 minutes or until the fish flakes easily.

Serves 4

Asiago-Encrusted Walleye

1	small onion, finely diced	1	pinch of cayenne pepper
1/2	small green bell pepper, chopped	3	tablespoons lemon juice
		1/2	cup bread crumbs
1/2	small red bell pepper, chopped	3	ounces (3/4 cup) shredded Asiago cheese
1/2	cup (1 stick) butter	4	(8- to 10-ounce) walleye pike fillets
1 1/2	tablespoons Dijon mustard		Salt and pepper to taste

Sauté the onion, green bell pepper and red bell pepper in the butter in a skillet until tender. Add the mustard, cayenne pepper and lemon juice. Stir in the bread crumbs and cheese. Remove from the heat and set aside for 1 minute. Place the fish on a piece of foil. Add the salt and pepper. Broil 4 inches from the heat source for 5 minutes. Turn over the fish, spread evenly with the cheese mixture and broil for 5 minutes longer.

Serves 4

FISH
Among the fish found in the lakes and streams of Michigan are steelhead, coho, perch, salmon, rainbow trout, lake trout, brown trout, smallmouth bass, largemouth bass, and walleye. Fishing in the state of Michigan is not limited to the warmer months. Many fine anglers step out in the winter months to enjoy ice fishing as a sport.

Baked Stuffed Whitefish

2   cups bread cubes, cut into 1/4-inch pieces
1/4   cup chopped fresh parsley
1/4   cup minced onion
1/2   cup (1 stick) butter, melted
      Salt and pepper to taste
1   (2- to 3-pound) whitefish, boned

Place the bread cubes, parsley and onion in a bowl. Pour on half the butter and toss to coat. Add the salt and pepper. Generously brush the fish with the remaining butter and stuff with the bread mixture. Skewer the fish. Place in a 2-inch-deep baking dish. Pour the remaining butter over the fish. Bake at 325 degrees for 45 minutes. Remove the fish head and fins. Cut the fish crosswise 2 inches thick.

Serves 4

Mussels in Wine

3   dozen large mussels (about 3 pounds)
3   tablespoons olive oil
1   small onion, diced
2   garlic cloves, minced
1   (16-ounce) can tomatoes
3/4   cup dry white wine
1/4   teaspoon basil
2   tablespoons chopped fresh parsley

Clean the mussels with a stiff brush under cold water 30 minutes before serving; set aside. Heat a large Dutch oven over medium heat. Add the olive oil. Add the onion and garlic and cook until tender, stirring occasionally. Stir in the tomatoes, wine and basil. Bring to a boil. Add the mussels and return to a boil. Reduce the heat to low. Cover and simmer for 5 minutes, stirring occasionally. Sprinkle with the parsley. Spoon the mussels into a bowl with the broth. Serve with sliced crusty bread.

Serves 4

Between the Lakes

Baked Sea Scallops

2	pounds sea scallops	1/8	teaspoon garlic powder
1/2	cup white wine	6	tablespoons butter,
1	tablespoon lemon juice		melted
1	teaspoon Worcestershire		Lemon wedges
	sauce		

Place the scallops in a non-reactive bowl. Add the wine and lemon juice and mix well. Marinate, covered, in the refrigerator for 4 hours. Drain the scallops, discarding the marinade. Place the scallops in a baking dish. Combine the Worcestershire sauce, garlic powder and melted butter in a small bowl. Pour over the scallops. Bake at 400 degrees for 25 minutes. Garnish the scallops with lemon wedges.

Serves 6 to 8

Broiled Curried Sea Scallops

2	pounds sea scallops	1	teaspoon lemon juice
1/4	cup maple syrup	2	teaspoons curry powder
1/4	cup mustard		

Place the scallops on a broiler pan lined with foil. Combine the maple syrup, mustard, lemon juice and curry powder in a bowl and mix well. Brush the tops of the scallops with half the curry mixture. Broil the scallops at the lowest level of the broiler for 10 minutes. Remove the scallops from the oven. Turn over the scallops and brush with the remaining curry mixture. Broil for 10 minutes longer.

Serves 5 to 6

Low Country Shrimp and Sausage Roast

Shrimp Marinade (see below)

12 to 14 large shrimp, unpeeled

4 to 8 red potatoes, unpeeled, cut into large pieces

1 pound carrots, cut into large pieces

2 onions, cut into wedges

10 garlic cloves, peeled

Salt and freshly ground pepper to taste

1 tablespoon chopped fresh rosemary

Olive oil for drizzling

1 pound smoked sausage, cut into large pieces

1 red bell pepper, cut into large pieces

Rosemary sprigs

Combine the Shrimp Marinade and shrimp in a sealable plastic bag. Marinate in the refrigerator for at least 1 hour. Combine the potatoes, carrots, onions, garlic, salt, pepper and rosemary in a large roasting pan. Drizzle on olive oil and toss to coat. Roast at 350 degrees for 30 minutes. Stir in the sausage and roast for 15 minutes. Add the bell pepper and roast for 10 minutes. Stir in the shrimp and the marinade and roast for 8 to 10 minutes or until the shrimp turn pink. Pour the shrimp mixture into a large bowl and garnish with rosemary sprigs. Serve with a crusty bread.

Serves 4

Shrimp Marinade

1 tablespoon olive oil

1 garlic clove, minced

1/2 cup parsley, chopped

1/2 teaspoon chopped fresh rosemary

Salt and pepper to taste

Combine the olive oil, garlic, parsley, rosemary, salt and pepper in a large bowl and mix well.

Saginaw Spaghetti

8   ounces thin spaghetti
1/4 cup (1/2 stick) butter or margarine
1/4 cup flour
1   cup chicken broth
1   cup heavy cream
1/3 cup shredded Gruyère or Swiss cheese
2   tablespoons sherry
     Dash of white pepper
1   (6-ounce) can sliced mushrooms,
     drained
1 1/2 pounds shrimp, cooked and peeled
1/3 cup grated Parmesan cheese
     Toasted slivered almonds (optional)

Cook the pasta using the package directions until al dente; drain. Melt the butter in a large saucepan. Blend in the flour. Gradually add the broth and cream. Cook over low heat until the sauce thickens, stirring constantly. Blend in the Gruyère cheese, sherry and pepper. Heat until the cheese melts, stirring frequently. Add the mushrooms. Remove from the heat and stir in the shrimp. Add the spaghetti. Remove the spaghetti mixture to a shallow 1 1/2-quart baking dish. Sprinkle with the Parmesan cheese. Broil 3 to 4 inches from the heat source for 5 to 7 minutes or until lightly browned. Sprinkle with the almonds.

Serves 6

Scrumptious Spinach Lasagna

16   ounces cottage cheese or
     ricotta cheese
1/4 cup (1 ounce) grated Parmesan cheese
1   (10-ounce) package frozen chopped
     spinach, thawed and squeezed dry
     Salt to taste
2   eggs
1   (32-ounce) jar spaghetti sauce
8   ounces lasagna noodles, cooked
     and drained
8   to 16 ounces (2 to 4 cups)
     mozzarella cheese, shredded
1/4 cup (1 ounce) grated Parmesan cheese

Combine the cottage cheese, 1/4 cup Parmesan cheese, spinach, salt and eggs in a large bowl and mix well. Spread a thin layer of spaghetti sauce on the bottom of a 9×13-inch baking dish. Layer the noodles, cottage cheese mixture, mozzarella cheese and remaining spaghetti sauce 1/2 at a time in the prepared dish. Sprinkle with 1/4 cup Parmesan cheese. Bake at 350 degrees for 1 hour. Remove from the oven and let stand for 15 minutes before serving.

Serves 8 to 10

111

Pasta Bows with Roasted Pepper Sauce

1   (7-ounce) jar roasted red peppers, drained
1/3   cup olive oil
1/3   cup grated Parmesan cheese
1/4   cup fresh basil
2   garlic cloves
1/8   teaspoon freshly ground pepper
1   teaspoon salt
12   ounces bow tie pasta (farfalle)
1   pound peeled cooked shrimp (optional)

Purée the red peppers, olive oil, cheese, basil, garlic, pepper and salt in a blender or food processor. Cook the pasta using the package directions until al dente; drain. Toss the pasta with the sauce. Stir in the shrimp.

Serves 4

Roasted Pheasant

Flour for dusting
Salt and pepper to taste
1   pheasant
2   tablespoons butter
2   tablespoons vegetable oil
1   apple, cut up
1/2   cup red wine
1   cup chicken broth
1/2   cup sour cream

Combine flour, salt and pepper on a plate. Dust the pheasant with the seasoned flour. Heat the butter and oil in a large skillet. Add the pheasant and brown. Remove the pheasant to a roasting pan. Add the apple. Add the wine to the skillet and simmer briefly, scraping up any browned bits. Pour the drippings into the roasting pan. Add the broth to the roasting pan and simmer 5 for minutes on top of the stove. Bake, covered, at 375 degrees for 30 minutes. Reduce the oven temperature to 350 degrees and roast for 1 hour longer. Let the pheasant stand for 10 minutes before carving. Stir the sour cream into the pan drippings to make a gravy. Serve the pheasant with the sour cream gravy.

Serves 2 or 3

Between the Lakes

Pheasant and Smoked Sausage Gumbo

1	cup vegetable oil	2	bay leaves	
1	cup flour	1/2	teaspoon thyme	
2	onions, chopped	1	fresh or dried cayenne pepper	
3	ribs celery, diced			
1	large green bell pepper, chopped	2	to 4 garlic cloves, crushed	
10	cups chicken broth	1	pound andouille sausage or smoked Polish sausage, sliced 1/4 inch thick	
6	boned pheasant breasts, chopped, or 1 (4-pound) chicken, cut into 8 pieces			
1	teaspoon salt	2	cups hot cooked rice	
1/2	teaspoon pepper (see note)			

WATERFOWL
Every year more than 5 million waterfowl, as well as even greater numbers of other migratory birds, pass through the Great Lakes region in the fall and spring. Michigan's varied outdoor environments make ideal roosting spots for numerous types of birds. Hunters enjoy the challenges posed by shooting wild turkey, pheasant, duck, geese, and partridge throughout the Great Lakes State.

Heat the oil in a tall heavy stockpot. Stir in the flour. Brown the oil and flour over medium heat to make a dark roux, stirring constantly. Do not let the mixture scorch. When the roux is the color of pecans, reduce the heat and add the onions, celery and bell pepper. Cook for 10 to 15 minutes. Add the chicken broth and pheasant. Bring to a boil; reduce the heat. Add the salt, pepper, bay leaves, thyme, cayenne pepper and garlic. Cook over medium heat for 1 hour. Add the sausage and cook for 1 hour longer. Remove the bay leaves and cayenne pepper. Serve the gumbo over the rice.

Note: If a whole cayenne pepper isn't available, substitute 1/2 teaspoon cayenne pepper. If using bone-in chicken remove after 1 hour. Discard the bones and return the chicken to the pot.

Serves 8

Pheasant and Mushrooms

    2   pheasants, cut into serving pieces
    1/2   cup pancake mix
    1/2   cup (1 stick) butter
    2   cups mushrooms, sliced
    1   small onion, chopped
    2   chicken bouillon cubes
    1   cup hot water
           Juice of 1/2 lemon
    1   teaspoon salt
    1   teaspoon pepper

Dust the pheasant with pancake mix in a shallow bowl. Melt the butter in a large skillet. Add the pheasant and sauté until brown. Remove the pheasant. Add the mushrooms and onion and sauté until brown. Dissolve the bouillon cubes in the hot water. Return the pheasant to the skillet. Add the bouillon, lemon juice, salt and pepper. Cook, covered, over low heat for 1 hour or until tender.

Serves 6 to 8

Venison Stroganoff

1   (10-ounce) can French onion soup
1   (10-ounce) can cream of mushroom soup
1   (10-ounce) can cream of celery soup
1   (10-ounce) can cream of chicken soup
1   (4-ounce) can mushrooms
2   to 3 pounds venison or sirloin steaks, cut into strips
    Cooked noodles or rice (optional)

Combine the onion soup, mushroom soup, celery soup, chicken soup and mushrooms in a heavy Dutch oven. Add the venison. Bake at 300 degrees for 3 hours. Serve over noodles.

Serves 8

VENISON
Venison is a naturally lean meat with very little fat cover. When preparing venison for cooking, as much fat, tallow, and silver skin as possible should be trimmed off. However, your recipe should provide some replacement to enhance the flavor. Butter, bacon strips, cheese, and even larding with beef fat will help. Don't overcook venison.

Lake Superior Cooking

Michigan is gorgeous and cooking on the shores of Lake Superior is out of this world. One pot meals, such as the one below, make it very easy. And then there is dessert. Bake a frozen blueberry pie in a Coleman oven on the shores of Lake Superior in a violent rain and wind storm, with pants rolled up, no shoes, tents going down on all sides, a martini in one hand and a pot holder in the other. Now that's good eating!

One Pot Chicken Dinner

1	can whole chicken	2	cups chicken broth
	Canned vegetables as		Salt and pepper to taste
	desired, such as carrots,	1	package baking mix
	potatoes, green beans		
	or onions		

*R*emove the chicken bones. Place the chicken and can liquids in a 4-quart kettle. Add the canned vegetables, chicken broth, salt and pepper. Heat the chicken mixture. Prepare dumplings using the directions on the package of the baking mix. Add the dumplings to the chicken and simmer until the dumplings are cooked through.

Serves about 8

Pot Roast Dinner

1	(10-ounce) can	1	envelope dried onion
	mushroom soup		soup mix
1	pot roast		

*P*our the mushroom soup on a large piece of heavy-duty foil. Place the pot roast on the foil. Top with the onion soup mix. Loosely wrap the pot roast. Place on a grill rack. Grill for 1 hour or to the desired degree of doneness.

Serves 8

Between the Lakes

Side Dishes

Artichoke Flan
Asparagus with Basil Vinaigrette
Asparagus and Carrot Sauté
Patio Beans
Christmas Broccoli
Maple Baked Carrots and Apples
Carrot Soufflé
Carrot Mushroom Pilaf
Corn and Cheese Soufflé
Ratatouille
Baked Morel Mushrooms
Vidalia Onion Classic Casserole
Deep-Fried Onion Rings
Dirty Mashed Potatoes
Hash Brown Potato Casserole
Ranch Potatoes
Sweet Potato Soufflé
Potato Gratin with Spinach and Onions
Spinach and Artichoke Casserole
Baked Spiced Butternut Squash
Tomatoes Stuffed with Orzo
Tomato Pie
Grilled and Baked Vegetables
Marvelous Mustard Mousse
Old-Fashioned Macaroni and Cheese
Christmas Pickles
Wild Rice Casserole
Pineapple Bake

Side Dishes

Artichoke Flan

1   (1-crust) pie pastry
1   egg white
1   (9-ounce) package frozen artichoke hearts, or 1 (14-ounce) can artichoke hearts, drained
3   eggs, lightly beaten
1 1/2   cups heavy cream
1 1/2   cups (6 ounces) shredded Swiss cheese
1/2   teaspoon salt
1/4   teaspoon thyme
     Dash of red pepper

Unfold the pastry into a 9-inch pie plate. Remove the plastic wrap. Fit the pastry into the plate. Fold the edges under and crimp. Brush the pie shell with egg white and set aside.

Cook the frozen artichoke hearts according to package directions; drain well. Combine the eggs, cream, cheese, salt, thyme and red pepper in a bowl and mix well. Pour the cheese mixture into the pie shell. Arrange the artichoke hearts over the filling. Bake at 375 degrees for 45 minutes or until a knife inserted in the center comes out clean.

Serves 8

Asparagus with Basil Vinaigrette

2   tablespoons chopped fresh basil
2   tablespoons olive oil
2   tablespoons vinegar
1/2   teaspoon salt
1/4   teaspoon sugar
1/8   teaspoon pepper
1   pound asparagus, trimmed
1/3   cup chopped tomato

Combine the basil, olive oil, vinegar, salt, sugar and pepper in a small bowl and chill in the refrigerator.

Steam the asparagus until tender-crisp; drain. Place the asparagus on a serving platter and spoon on the dressing and chopped tomato.

Serves 4

Asparagus and Carrot Sauté

2   pounds thin asparagus
10 ounces thin carrots, peeled
2   tablespoons unsalted butter
1   tablespoon vegetable oil
2   green onions, minced
     Generous pinch of marjoram
     Generous pinch of chervil
     Salt and freshly ground pepper
     to taste

Cut the asparagus diagonally into 1/2-inch slices, reserving the tips. Slice the carrots into halves lengthwise and then diagonally into 1/2-inch slices. Melt the butter and oil in a large skillet or wok over medium-high heat. Add the carrots and sauté for 3 minutes. Add the asparagus stems and sauté for 1 minute. Add the asparagus tips and cook for 1 minute, stirring constantly. Stir in the green onions, marjoram, chervil, salt and pepper and cook briefly to blend the flavors.

Serves 4

Patio Beans

4   slices bacon
1   onion, chopped
1   (2-pound) jar Randall Mixed Beans
4   ounces cubed sharp Cheddar cheese
1/2 cup packed brown sugar
1/3 cup ketchup
     Worcestershire sauce to taste
     Freshly grated Parmesan cheese

Place the bacon in a skillet and cook over medium-high heat until the bacon is crisp-cooked. Remove the bacon with a slotted spoon and drain on paper towels. Add the onion to the bacon drippings and sauté for a few minutes until transparent.

Combine the beans, Cheddar cheese, brown sugar, ketchup and Worcestershire sauce in a large bowl. Stir in the onion and bacon. Spoon into a baking dish or ovenproof Dutch oven. Sprinkle with Parmesan cheese. Bake at 350 degrees for 30 to 45 minutes or until the mixture is heated through and bubbly.

Serves 8

Christmas Broccoli

2   tablespoons butter
1/2 large onion, chopped
2   (10-ounce) packages frozen
     chopped broccoli
1   (10-ounce) can mushroom soup
1/2 (5-ounce) jar Old English cheese
     spread
1   garlic clove, pressed
1   (4-ounce) can sliced mushrooms
1   (2-ounce) jar chopped pimentos
1/4 cup bread crumbs
1/4 cup slivered almonds

Melt the butter in a small skillet. Add the onion. Sauté until golden and set aside.

Cook the broccoli according to package directions; drain. Combine the soup, cheese spread, garlic and onion in a bowl and mix well. Add the mushrooms, pimentos and broccoli and mix well. Spoon the broccoli mixture into a baking dish. Sprinkle with the bread crumbs and almonds. Bake at 350 degrees for 20 minutes.

Serves 6

Maple Baked Carrots and Apples

     Salt to taste
4   large carrots, peeled and sliced
2   apples, peeled and thinly sliced
2   tablespoons maple syrup
2   tablespoons brown sugar
2   tablespoons butter or margarine

Bring enough salted water to cover the carrots to a boil in a saucepan. Add the carrots. Cook until tender-crisp; drain. Combine the carrots and apple slices in a bowl. Stir in the maple syrup and brown sugar. Spoon the carrot mixture into a buttered 1 1/2-quart baking dish. Dot with the butter. Bake at 375 degrees for 1 hour or until the apples are tender, stirring once or twice during baking.

Serves 4 to 6

Carrot Soufflé

7	cups chopped carrots (about 2 pounds)
1/4	cup fat-free sour cream
2/3	cup sugar
3	tablespoons flour
2	tablespoons butter, melted
1	teaspoon baking powder
1	teaspoon vanilla extract
1/4	teaspoon salt
3	eggs, lightly beaten
1	teaspoon confectioners' sugar

Bring enough water to cover the carrots to a boil in a saucepan. Add the carrots and cook until very tender; drain. Purée the carrots and sour cream in a blender. Add the sugar, flour, melted butter, baking powder, vanilla, salt and eggs. Pulse to combine.

Spoon the carrot mixture into a 2-quart baking dish sprayed with nonstick cooking spray. Bake at 350 degrees for 40 minutes or until puffed and set. Remove the soufflé from the oven and dust with confectioners' sugar.

Serves 8

Carrot Mushroom Pilaf

1/4	cup (1/2 stick) unsalted butter	8	ounces mushrooms, sliced
1	bunch green onions, chopped	3/4	cup chopped fresh Italian parsley
3	carrots, peeled and chopped	1/4	teaspoon pepper
2	cups brown rice	2	eggs, beaten
41/2	cups chicken broth	1	cup half-and-half
1/2	cup dry white wine	1/2	teaspoon ground nutmeg
1/4	cup (1/2 stick) unsalted butter	1	cup (4 ounces) grated Parmesan cheese, or to taste
2	garlic cloves, minced	1/4	cup chopped green onions (optional)

Melt 1/4 cup butter in a large skillet. Add the green onions and carrots. Sauté for 5 minutes or until tender. Add the rice and cook for 1 minute, stirring constantly. Stir in the chicken broth and wine. Bring to a boil. Cover, reduce the heat and simmer for 45 minutes or until the liquid is absorbed and the rice is tender. Set aside.

Melt 1/4 cup butter in a small skillet. Add the garlic and cook for 1 minute. Stir in the mushrooms. Cook for 5 minutes and drain. Stir in the parsley and pepper. Combine the eggs, half-and-half and nutmeg in a bowl and mix well. Set aside. Layer half the rice mixture, mushrooms and half the cheese in the bottom of a lightly greased 9×13-inch baking pan. Cover with the remaining rice mixture and sprinkle with the remaining 1/2 cup cheese. Pour the egg mixture over the top. Bake at 350 degrees for 30 to 40 minutes or until heated through. Sprinkle with 1/4 cup chopped green onions.

Note: This dish can be assembled in advance and refrigerated. Bring to room temperature before baking.

Serves 8

CARROTS

One carrot has 40 calories and is high in fiber, potassium, and vitamin A. If protected from heat and light, carrots will increase in vitamin A for up to five months in storage. When shopping for carrots, look for an orange-yellow color, firmness, and crisp, green tops. The tops should be trimmed and the carrots stored in a cool, dark, and ventilated area to prevent formation of chemical compounds which produce a bitter taste.

Corn and Cheese Soufflé

1   cup hot milk
1 1/2 cups soft bread crumbs
1 1/2 cups (6 ounces) shredded Cheddar
     cheese
1   (17-ounce) can cream-style corn
2   tablespoons butter or margarine,
     melted
1/2   teaspoon salt
1/4   teaspoon pepper
3   eggs, separated

Combine the milk, bread crumbs,
cheese, corn, melted butter, salt and pepper
in a large bowl and mix well. Beat the egg
yolks in a small bowl until thick and stir
into the corn mixture. Beat the egg whites
at high speed in a mixing bowl until stiff
but not dry. Fold the egg whites into the
corn mixture. Pour into a greased 2-quart
baking dish or soufflé dish. Bake at 400
degrees for 45 minutes or until a knife
inserted in the center comes out clean.

Serves 4

Ratatouille

3   tablespoons olive oil
1   onion, chopped
2   garlic cloves, minced
1   each green and yellow bell pepper,
     cut lengthwise into 1/4-inch strips
1/2   red bell pepper, cut lengthwise into
     1/4-inch strips
1   eggplant, sliced 1/4 inch thick
1   cup thinly sliced mushrooms
3   tablespoons olive oil
     Salt and freshly ground pepper to taste
3   large tomatoes, cut into halves
     lengthwise and sliced crosswise
     1/3 inch thick
1/3   cup fresh basil, chopped
2/3   cup (2 1/2 ounces) coarsely grated
     Romano cheese or Parmesan cheese

Heat 3 tablespoons olive oil in large
heavy non-reactive skillet over moderately
high heat. Add the onion, garlic, green
bell pepper, yellow bell pepper, red bell
pepper, eggplant and mushrooms. Sauté
for 15 minutes or until the vegetables
soften, tossing the vegetables and adding
3 tablespoons oil as necessary. Stir in the
salt, pepper, basil and tomatoes. Cook for
1 minute. Remove the vegetables to a
14-inch oval gratin dish and top with the
cheese. Cover the dish with foil. Bake at
400 degrees for 30 minutes or until the
vegetables are very tender. Serve the dish
hot, warm or cold.

Serves 8

Between the Lakes

Baked Morel Mushrooms

1	pound morel mushrooms, cut into halves
1/2	cup (1 stick) butter, melted
1	tablespoon chopped fresh chives
1/2	teaspoon marjoram
1/4	teaspoon salt
	Pepper to taste
1/4	cup dry sherry
1/2	cup chicken broth
4	thin slices of buttered toast, cut into quarters

Combine the mushrooms, butter, chives, marjoram, salt, pepper, sherry and chicken broth in a 1 1/2-quart baking dish. Cover with foil. Bake at 350 degrees for 20 minutes. Place the toast in a small bowl. Ladle the hot mushrooms and broth over the toast.

Serves 8

Vidalia Onion Classic Casserole

1/2	cup (1 stick) butter or margarine
4	large Vidalia onions, cut into 1/2-inch slices
2/3	cup chicken broth
1/3	cup sherry
2	tablespoons flour
1 1/2	cups soft bread crumbs
1/2	cup (2 ounces) shredded Cheddar cheese
2	tablespoons grated Parmesan cheese

Melt the butter in a large skillet. Add the onions and sauté until tender. Add the chicken broth, sherry and flour and mix well. Remove to a medium baking dish. Top with the bread crumbs, Cheddar cheese and Parmesan cheese. Bake at 350 degrees for 20 to 30 minutes or until browned.

Serves 6 to 8

MOREL MUSHROOMS

Morels are among the most highly prized of all the wild mushrooms. Morels are flavorful and need little embellishment—simply sauté in butter or light oil. The key is to keep them cool and dry with a little ventilation. Do not store refrigerated in a sealed plastic bag.

Deep-Fried Onion Rings

1   large sweet white onion (about 1 1/4 pounds)
4   cups (1 quart) buttermilk
     Vegetable oil for deep-frying (about 6 cups)
1 1/2 cups flour
1/4   cup stone-ground yellow cornmeal
1 1/2 teaspoons coarse salt plus extra for sprinkling if desired
1   teaspoon freshly ground pepper
1   tablespoon smoky chili powder (optional)

Peel the onion and slice 1/3 inch thick. Separate the slices into rings. Soak the onion rings in the buttermilk in a large bowl for 30 minutes, stirring occasionally. Heat the oil in a large kettle over moderately high heat to 375 degrees. Mix the flour, cornmeal, coarse salt, pepper and chili powder on a plate. Coat the onion rings 1 at a time with the flour mixture. Place 5 or 6 onion rings at a time in the hot oil. Fry for 2 to 3 minutes or until golden brown, turning over once. Remove the onion rings and drain on paper towels. Season with additional salt. Serve hot.

Serves 6

Between the Lakes

Dirty Mashed Potatoes

6 to 8 red potatoes, scrubbed and halved
3 parsnips, peeled and cut into large chunks
2 large carrots, peeled and cut into large chunks
Salt and pepper to taste
2 tablespoons sour cream
Butter to taste
Milk (optional)

Combine the potatoes, parsnips and carrots with enough water to cover in a saucepan. Bring to a boil. Boil until tender; drain. Mash the potatoes, parsnips, carrots, salt, pepper, sour cream and butter together in a bowl. Add enough milk for the desired consistency.

Serves 8

Hash Brown Potato Casserole

2 pounds frozen hash brown potatoes
1 cup finely chopped onion
1 (10-ounce) can cream of chicken soup
1/2 cup (1 stick) margarine, melted
2 cups sour cream
8 ounces shredded Cheddar cheese
Salt and pepper to taste
5 cups crushed cornflakes
1/3 cup margarine, melted

Combine the potatoes, onion, chicken soup, 1/2 cup margarine, sour cream, cheese, salt and pepper in a large bowl and mix well. Spoon the potato mixture into a 9×13-inch baking dish. Toss the cornflakes with 1/3 cup margarine in a bowl and spread over the potato mixture. Bake at 350 degrees for 1 hour.

Serves 10

POTATOES
The nation's largest producer of summer ("new") potatoes and potatoes for chip manufacturing is found right here in the Great Lakes State of Michigan. A medium potato has 76 calories—no more than an apple. Potatoes are fat-free, rich in potassium and an excellent source of fiber. A potato contains one-half the daily requirement of vitamin C, 15% of the recommended daily allowance of vitamin B6, and 10% of the niacin requirements.

Ranch Potatoes

20   small to medium red new potatoes,
       scrubbed and cubed
1   large onion, chopped
8   slices bacon, cut into 1-inch pieces
3   garlic cloves, minced
2   tablespoons olive oil
1   envelope ranch salad dressing mix
       Freshly ground pepper to taste

Place the potatoes in a 10×13-inch baking dish brushed with olive oil. Add the onion, bacon, garlic and 2 tablespoons olive oil and mix together. Sprinkle with the ranch salad dressing mix and pepper and mix well. Bake at 350 degrees for 2 hours or until well browned and crisp, stirring occasionally.

Serves 10

Sweet Potato Soufflé

4   very large sweet potatoes
1   tablespoon vanilla extract
1/4   cup milk
1/4   cup (1/2 stick) butter
1   cup packed brown sugar
1/3   cup butter, melted
1/2   cup quick-cooking oats
1/2   cup flour
1/3   cup pecans, chopped

Pierce the sweet potatoes and bake at 450 degrees for 1 1/2 hours or until soft. Peel the sweet potatoes. Mash the sweet potatoes with vanilla, milk and 1/4 cup butter in a large bowl. Spoon into a buttered 2-quart baking dish. Bake at 350 degrees for 15 to 20 minutes. Combine the brown sugar, 1/3 cup butter, oats, flour and pecans in a bowl and mix well. Spread over the sweet potato mixture and bake for 15 minutes longer.

Serves 8 to 10

Between the Lakes

Potato Gratin with Spinach and Onions

1³/4 pounds Yukon Gold
  potatoes
  Salt to taste
2 large onions, cut into
  halves and thinly sliced
1/4 cup water
2 tablespoons extra-virgin
  olive oil
8 ounces mushrooms,
  thinly sliced
1 (10-ounce) package
  frozen chopped spinach,
  thawed and drained

4 garlic cloves, minced
4 teaspoons chopped
  fresh thyme
1/4 teaspoon nutmeg
1 cup nonfat sour cream
1/2 cup reduced-fat milk
  Pepper to taste
2 ounces Gruyère cheese,
  thinly sliced

Combine the potatoes with enough salted water to cover in a saucepan. Bring to a boil. Boil for 30 minutes or until tender; drain and cool. Slice the potatoes 1/3 inch thick, removing any loose peel. Set aside. Combine the onions and water in a large non-reactive skillet. Cover and simmer for 12 minutes or until the onions are tender, stirring occasionally and adding more water by the tablespoonful if the onions are dry. Increase the heat to medium-high. Add the olive oil and mushrooms. Sauté for 10 minutes or until the onions are deep golden brown. Add the spinach, garlic, thyme and nutmeg. Cook for 3 minutes, stirring constantly. Remove from the heat. Stir in the sour cream, milk, salt and pepper.

Layer half the potatoes overlapping slightly in a lightly oiled 7×11-inch glass baking dish. Season with salt and pepper. Layer half the spinach mixture over the potatoes. Continue layering the remaining potatoes and spinach mixture over the layers. Top with the cheese. Bake at 350 degrees for 30 minutes or until hot and bubbly. Let stand for 5 minutes before serving.

Serves 10

Spinach and Artichoke Casserole

2   (10-ounce) packages frozen
     chopped spinach
1   (8-ounce) package cream cheese,
     softened
1/2 cup (1 stick) butter, melted
1   (4-ounce) can artichokes, drained
     and quartered
1   (8-ounce) can sliced water chestnuts,
     drained
1   teaspoon Worcestershire sauce
2   tablespoons lemon juice
     Dash of Tabasco sauce
     Salt and pepper to taste
1/4 to 1/2 cup (2 to 4 ounces) grated
     Parmesan cheese

Cook the spinach using the package directions and squeeze dry. Set aside. Combine the cream cheese and melted butter in a bowl and mix well. Add the spinach, artichokes and water chestnuts. Stir in the Worcestershire sauce, lemon juice, Tabasco sauce, salt and pepper. Spoon the spinach mixture into a 2-quart baking dish. Sprinkle with the cheese. Bake at 350 degrees for 40 minutes.

Serves 6

Baked Spiced Butternut Squash

1/2 cup (1 stick) butter
3/4 cup maple syrup
1/4 cup apple juice
1   teaspoon cinnamon
1/2 teaspoon each ground allspice and salt
3   small butternut squash
4   Granny Smith apples
     Salt and pepper to taste

Combine the butter, maple syrup and apple juice in a saucepan and mix well. Cook over medium heat until the butter melts, stirring occasionally. Increase the heat and cook for 5 minutes or until the mixture is slightly reduced. Remove from the heat and stir in the cinnamon, allspice and 1/2 teaspoon salt.

Peel the squash and cut into halves lengthwise, discarding the seeds. Cut each half crosswise into slices 1/4 inch thick. Peel the apples and cut into halves. Cut each half into slices 1/4 inch thick. Spread 1/3 of the squash slices in a buttered 9×13-inch glass baking dish. Continue layering with 1/2 of the apples and 1/2 of the remaining squash. Alternate the remaining apple and squash slices on top and season with salt and pepper. Pour the maple syrup mixture over the layers and cover tightly with foil. Bake at 400 degrees for 50 minutes or until the squash is tender. Uncover the dish and bake 20 minutes longer, basting occasionally with the maple syrup mixture.

Serves 8 to 10

Between the Lakes

Tomatoes Stuffed with Orzo

1 cup orzo
6 large tomatoes
1 (14- to 15-ounce) jar spaghetti sauce
1 small onion, finely chopped
2 tablespoons olive oil
1 (10-ounce) package frozen chopped spinach, thawed and squeezed dry
1 cup (4 ounces) shredded Cheddar cheese
1 cup (4 ounces) shredded mozzarella cheese
1/4 teaspoon salt
1/4 teaspoon pepper

Cook the orzo using the package directions until al dente, omitting the salt; drain and place in a large bowl. Cut a thin slice off the tops of the tomatoes. Scoop out and dice the pulp, reserving the tomato shells. Spread the tomato pulp in an 8×12-inch glass or ceramic baking dish. Add the spaghetti sauce and mix well. Sauté the onion in the olive oil in a small skillet until slightly brown. Add the onion, spinach, Cheddar cheese, mozzarella cheese, salt and pepper to the orzo and mix well. Mound the orzo mixture into the reserve tomato shells. Place the tomato shells in the sauce. Cover with a foil tent. Bake at 375 degrees for 1 hour or until the sauce is hot and the orzo is heated through.

Serves 6

Tomato Pie

6 to 8 large tomatoes, peeled, seeded and thickly sliced
2 or 3 green onions, chopped
1 baked (9-inch) deep pie shell
  Salt and pepper to taste
10 basil leaves, finely chopped
5 chives, chopped
1 cup mayonnaise
1 cup (4 ounces) shredded sharp Cheddar cheese
3 slices bacon, crisp-cooked and crumbled
  Parmesan cheese to taste

Layer the tomato slices and green onions in the pie shell. Sprinkle with the salt, pepper, basil and chives. Stir together the mayonnaise and Cheddar cheese in a small bowl and spread over the tomatoes. Top with the bacon and Parmesan cheese. Bake at 350 degrees for 30 minutes.

Note: To peel the tomatoes, scald in boiling water for 1 minute; drain. Dip the tomatoes in a bowl of ice water.

Serves 8

Grilled and Baked Vegetables

Olive oil for brushing
1   eggplant, sliced 1/8 to 1/4 inch thick
1   yellow summer squash, sliced 1/8 to 1/4 inch thick
1   zucchini, sliced 1/8 to 1/4 inch thick
1   onion, sliced 1/8 to 1/4 inch thick
1   each red, yellow and green bell peppers, sliced 1/8 to 1/4 inch thick
2   or 3 Roma tomatoes, peeled and chopped
1   tablespoon olive oil
     Salt and pepper to taste
1   or 2 garlic cloves, finely chopped
1/4 to 1/2 cup freshly grated Parmesan cheese

Heat a grill pan brushed with olive oil over high heat. Add the eggplant and grill until tender. Remove to a wide, shallow baking dish. Repeat with the summer squash, zucchini, onion and bell peppers. Top the vegetables with chopped tomatoes. Add 1 tablespoon olive oil, salt, pepper and garlic. Top with the cheese. Bake at 400 degrees for 15 to 20 minutes or until the cheese is golden.

Serves 8

Marvelous Mustard Mousse

1   envelope unflavored gelatin
1/4 cup lemon juice
4   eggs, beaten
2/3 cup sugar
1/2 cup water
1/2 cup cider vinegar
3   tablespoons Dijon mustard
1/4 teaspoon salt
1   cup whipping cream, whipped
2   tablespoons minced fresh parsley

Soften the gelatin in lemon juice in a small bowl; let stand for 5 minutes. Combine the eggs, sugar, water, vinegar, mustard and salt in a medium saucepan. Add the gelatin mixture. Cook over medium heat until the mixture thickens; do not boil. Chill, covered, for 1 hour or until the mustard mixture is thick and almost set. Whisk the mixture until smooth. Fold in the whipped cream and parsley. Spoon the mustard mixture into a well-oiled 4-cup mold. Chill, covered, for 8 to 12 hours. Unmold and serve.

Serves 8

Between the Lakes

Old-Fashioned Macaroni and Cheese

2	cups elbow macaroni	2	tablespoons butter or
2	tablespoons grated onion		margarine
1	teaspoon salt	2	tablespoons flour
1/4	teaspoon pepper	1/2	teaspoon salt
3	cups (12 ounces)	1/4	teaspoon pepper
	shredded sharp	2	cups milk
	American cheese	1	tablespoon butter

Cook the macaroni using the package directions until al dente; drain. Place half the macaroni in a 2-quart baking dish. Layer with half the onion, 1/4 teaspoon of the salt, 1/8 teaspoon of the pepper and cheese. Repeat the layers.

Melt 2 tablespoons butter in a medium saucepan over low heat. Stir in the flour, remaining salt and pepper. Cook over low heat until the mixture is smooth and starting to bubble, stirring frequently. Remove from the heat. Stir in the milk. Heat to boiling and cook for 1 minute, stirring constantly. Pour over the macaroni. Dot with the remaining butter. Cover the dish. Bake at 375 degrees for 30 minutes. Uncover and bake for 15 minutes longer.

Serves 6

Christmas Pickles

1	(1-quart) jar dill pickles	3	tablespoons vinegar
1 1/4	cups sugar	1	tablespoon prepared
1	onion, finely chopped		white horseradish
1	teaspoon celery seeds		

Drain the pickles. Slice the pickles into strips and return to the jar. Add the sugar, onion, celery seeds, vinegar and horseradish. Refrigerate, shaking often to dissolve the sugar.

Makes 1 quart

CRANBERRIES

Michigan's climate, soil and water resources make the state an excellent location for cranberry production. Pilgrims named the fruit "craneberry" for the small, pink blossoms that resemble the head and bill of a sandhill crane. Cranberries are a superior source of nutrition and vitamins, including vitamin C, and contain antioxidants, natural plant products that may protect against cancer, heart disease and other illnesses.

Wild Rice Casserole

This is a "dump ingredients" recipe. It looks unappealing until it's baked.

1	(6-ounce) package long-grain and wild rice with herbs and seasonings
1	(28-ounce) can whole tomatoes, undrained, chopped
1/2	cup chopped black olives
1	(4 ounce) can mushroom stems and pieces
1/2	cup vegetable oil or olive oil
1/2	cup chopped onion
1	teaspoon salt
1	teaspoon pepper
1	cup (4 ounces) mild Cheddar cheese, cubed
1 1/2	cups boiling water

Combine the rice, tomatoes, olives, mushrooms, oil, onion, salt and pepper in a large baking dish. Top with the cheese. Add the boiling water. Cover the dish. Bake at 350 degrees for 1 hour; uncover and bake for 30 minutes longer.

Serves 8

Pineapple Bake

1/2	cup (1 stick) butter
7	slices white bread, torn into coarse crumbs
1/4	cup sugar
2	eggs, lightly beaten
3	tablespoons flour
1	(20-ounce) can juice-pack crushed pineapple

Melt the butter in a large skillet. Add the bread crumbs and brown over medium heat. Whisk together the sugar, eggs and flour in a bowl. Stir in the pineapple. Pour the egg mixture into a 2-quart baking dish and cover with the bread crumbs. Press the crumbs down into the egg mixture, but do nor stir. Bake at 350 degrees for 45 minutes. Serve hot.

Serves 8

Between the Lakes

Desserts

Apple Cream Tart
Blueberry Pie
Grandma's Peach Pie
Coconut Pineapple Pie
Walnut Pie
French Bread Pudding with
Rum Sauce
Rum Sauce
Buñuelos
Sour Cream Cheesecake
Decadent Ice Cream Dessert
Frozen Oreo Dessert
Lemon Ice
Fresh Peach Cobbler
Raspberry Soufflé
Strawberry Shortcake Dessert
Summer Trifle Cake
Caramel and Banana Sauce
Da's Famous Fudge Sauce
Fresh Apple Cake with Caramel Glaze
Apple Cider Pound Cake
Brown Sugar Pound Cake
Banana Birthday Cake

Chocolate Chocolate Chip Cake
The Greatest Carrot Cake
Milky Way Swirl Cake
Orange Pour-Over Cake
Do-Nothing Pineapple Cake
Pumpkin Cake Roll
Best-Ever Rhubarb Cake
Rum Cake
Strawberry Treasure Cake
Michigan Nut and Berry Bark
Peanut Butter Crunch Bars
Animal Cookies
Disappearing Marshmallow Brownies
Chocolate Caramel Bars
Crème de Menthe Squares
Cream Cheese Cookies
Lemon Cheese Logs
Lemon Bars
Maple Cookies
Molasses Cookies
Pecan Pie Bars
Potato Chip Cookies
Sour Cream Cookies

Desserts

Apple Cream Tart

This is graciously shared by the Michigan Apple Committee.

4   cups sliced peeled Michigan apples
1/2   cup sugar
2   tablespoons flour
1/4   cup chopped walnuts
1/2   teaspoon cinnamon
1/3   cup nonfat sour cream
1   egg
2   tablespoons sugar
1   (1-crust) pie pastry

Combine the apples, 1/2 cup sugar, flour, walnuts and cinnamon in a bowl; set aside. Combine the sour cream, egg and 2 tablespoons sugar in a small bowl; set aside. Place the pie pastry on a 12-inch pizza pan and seal any cracks. Place the apple mixture in the center of the crust, leaving a 3-inch rim. Pull up the edges of the pie pastry, covering part of the apple filling. Pleat the pie pastry edge every 2 inches. Pour the sour cream mixture carefully over the apples. Bake at 375 degrees for 50 minutes or until the pastry is golden and the apples are tender. Serve warm or cold.

Note: Use Empire, Gala, Golden Delicious, Ida Red, Jonagold, Jonathan, McIntosh or Rome apples. If desired substitute one 21-ounce can apple pie filling for the apples, sugar and flour. Stir the cinnamon into the pie filling.

Serves 8

Blueberry Pie

1   heaping quart blueberries
2   teaspoons lemon juice
1   cup minus 2 tablespoons sugar
2   tablespoons plus 1 teaspoon flour
1/2 teaspoon cinnamon
1   (2-crust) pie pastry
3   to 4 tablespoons butter
     Sugar for sprinkling

Rinse the blueberries and drain well. Place the blueberries in a bowl and sprinkle with lemon juice. Combine 1 cup minus 2 tablespoons sugar, flour and cinnamon in a bowl and add to the blueberries. Line a deep 9-inch pie plate with half the pastry. Pour in half the blueberry mixture. Dot with half the butter. Top with the remaining blueberries and the remaining butter. Roll out the remaining pie pastry. Cut into strips 3/4-inch wide. Arrange lattice-fashion over the pie. Crimp the edges. Lightly sprinkle with sugar. Bake at 425 degrees for 15 minutes. Reduce the oven temperature to 350 degrees and bake for 35 to 40 minutes longer or until the top and bottom crusts are nicely browned and the center is bubbly.

Serves 8

Grandma's Peach Pie

2/3 cup sugar
1/3 cup packed brown sugar
1/2 teaspoon salt
3   tablespoons flour
1/4 teaspoon nutmeg
1/2 teaspoon cinnamon
1   teaspoon lemon juice
1/4 cup (1/2 stick) butter, softened
5   to 6 cups sliced peeled peaches
1   (2-crust) pie pastry
     Milk for brushing
     Sugar for sprinkling

Combine 2/3 cup sugar, brown sugar, salt, flour, nutmeg, cinnamon and lemon juice in a large bowl. Cut in the butter until crumbly. Add the peach slices and mix well. Fit one pie pastry into a 9-inch pie plate. Pour in the peach mixture. Top with the remaining pastry, sealing the edge and cutting vents. Brush the crust with milk and sprinkle with sugar. Bake at 425 degrees for 45 minutes. If the crust browns too much, place a crust shield or foil over the top.

Serves 8

Between the Lakes

Coconut Pineapple Pie

1	cup sugar	1	teaspoon vanilla extract
3	tablespoons flour	1/4	cup (1/2 stick)
1	cup corn syrup		margarine or butter,
1	cup flaked coconut		melted
1	(8-ounce) can crushed	1	unbaked (9-inch)
	pineapple		pie shell
3	eggs, beaten		

Mix the sugar and flour in a large bowl. Add the corn syrup, coconut, pineapple, eggs and vanilla and mix well. Add the butter. Pour the coconut mixture into the pie shell. Bake at 350 degrees for 50 to 55 minutes, covering with foil if the pie browns too quickly. Chill in the refrigerator before serving.

Serves 6 to 8

Walnut Pie

3	egg whites, at room	11	soda crackers, finely
	temperature		crushed
1	cup sugar	1	teaspoon baking powder
1	teaspoon vanilla extract	1/2	cup walnuts, chopped

Beat the egg whites in a mixing bowl until stiff peaks form. Add the sugar gradually beating until stiff peaks form. Beat in the vanilla. Combine the soda crackers and baking powder in a bowl. Fold the crackers into the egg whites. Fold in the walnuts. Spoon the walnut mixture into a greased 9-inch pie plate. Bake at 325 degrees for 45 minutes. Serve with ice cream and fudge sauce or fresh fruit.

Serves 6

BLUEBERRIES
USDA researchers have found that blueberries rank number one in antioxidant activity. Antioxidants help neutralize harmful by-products of metabolism called "free radicals" that can lead to cancer and other age-related diseases. When baking, in order to maximize flavor, blueberry muffins should contain 33% fruit. Michigan ranks number one in the production of high bush blueberries.

French Bread Pudding with Rum Sauce

1/2	cup (1 stick) butter, softened	6	egg yolks
1	cup sugar	1/2	cup sugar
5	eggs, beaten	6	egg whites, at room temperature
2	cups heavy cream		
	Dash of cinnamon	1/2	cup confectioners' sugar
1	tablespoon vanilla extract		Butter
1/4	cup raisins		Sugar
12	(1 inch thick) slices fresh or day-old French bread		Rum Sauce (page 141)

Cream the butter and 1 cup sugar together in a mixing bowl until light and fluffy. Add the beaten eggs, cream, cinnamon, vanilla and raisins and mix well. Pour into a 9×9-inch baking pan 13/4 inches deep. Arrange the bread slices in the egg mixture and let stand for 5 minutes to soak up some of the liquid. Turn the bread over and let stand for 10 minutes. Gently push the bread into the egg mixture; do not break the bread. Place the baking pan in a larger baking pan. Add water to the larger pan to 1/2 inch from the top. Cover the bread pudding with a sheet of foil. Bake at 350 degrees for 45 to 50 minutes, uncovering the pudding during the last 10 minutes to brown. The custard should be soft. Remove from the oven. Chill, covered, for 8 to 12 hours.

Place the egg yolks and 1/2 cup sugar in the top of a double boiler. Whip over simmering water until the egg yolks are frothy and shiny. Spoon the chilled bread pudding into a large bowl. Add the egg yolks and mix well. Beat the egg whites in a mixing bowl until frothy. Add the confectioners' sugar gradually, beating until stiff peaks form. Gently fold the egg whites into the bread pudding mixture. Butter and lightly sugar a 11/2-quart soufflé dish. Spoon the bread pudding into the dish filling 3/4 full. Wipe the lip of the soufflé dish clean. Bake at 375 degrees for 35 minutes. Remove the soufflé from the oven and serve immediately with the Rum Sauce on the side.

Serves 8 to 10

Rum Sauce

1   cup sugar
2   cups water
1   cinnamon stick, or 1 teaspoon ground
    cinnamon
1   tablespoon unsalted butter
1/2 teaspoon cornstarch
1/2 cup water
1   tablespoon light or dark rum

Combine the sugar, 2 cups water, cinnamon and butter in a medium saucepan and bring to a boil. Dissolve the cornstarch in 1/2 cup water. Stir into the boiling mixture. Simmer until the sauce is clear, stirring frequently. Remove from heat and add the rum. The sauce will be thin. Remove the cinnamon stick.

Serves 8 to 10

Buñuelos

4   cups flour
1   teaspoon salt
1   teaspoon baking powder
2   tablespoons sugar
2   large eggs
1   cup milk
1/3 cup butter, melted
    Vegetable oil for deep frying
1/2 cup sugar
2   teaspoons cinnamon

Sift the flour, salt, baking powder and 2 tablespoons sugar together into a bowl. Beat the eggs in a large bowl. Add the milk. Gradually stir in the dry ingredients. Add the melted butter, kneading into the dough by hand. Knead on a floured surface until smooth and elastic. Divide dough into 25 large or 40 small balls. Roll each ball into a thin 4-inch or 6-inch circle. Heat the oil in a large deep skillet. Add buñuelos a few at a time. Fry to light golden brown on both sides. Drain on paper towels. Combine 1/2 cup sugar and the cinnamon in a small bowl. Sprinkle on the buñuelos. Serve with coffee ice cream, Kahlúa and chopped toasted pecans.

Note: The dough can be made up to 3 days in advance, covered and refrigerated. Press the centers of the buñuelos with a ladle when frying to form small bowls if desired.

Serves 25 to 40

141

Sour Cream Cheesecake

Graham Cracker Crust (see below)
5   (8-ounce) packages cream cheese, softened
1 1/2   cups sugar
6   eggs
1   teaspoon vanilla extract
3   cups sour cream
1/3   cup sugar
1   teaspoon vanilla extract

Prepare the crust. Press firmly on the bottom and up the sides of a 10-inch springform pan. Set aside. Beat the cream cheese in a mixing bowl until smooth. Gradually add 1 1/2 cups sugar. Add the eggs 1 at a time, mixing well after each addition. Add the vanilla and mix well, scraping the bowl frequently. Pour the filling into the crust. Bake at 350 degrees for 50 to 60 minutes. Remove the cheesecake from the oven. Mix the sour cream, 1/3 cup sugar and 1 teaspoon vanilla together in a bowl. Spread over the cheesecake. Bake for 15 minutes longer. Cool completely. Chill, covered, until ready to serve.

Serves 16

Graham Cracker Crust

1 3/4   cups graham cracker crumbs
2/3   cup sugar
1/2   cup (1 stick) unsalted butter, softened

Combine the cracker crumbs and sugar in a bowl. Add the butter and mix well.

Decadent Ice Cream Dessert

1 1/4 cups Oreos, crushed
3   tablespoons butter or margarine
1   (12-ounce) jar caramel sauce
1   quart chocolate ice cream, softened
1   quart vanilla ice cream, softened
6   toffee candy bars, broken up
1   (10-ounce) jar Swiss chocolate sauce
1   quart coffee ice cream, softened

Combine the Oreos and butter in a bowl. Press into a 10-inch springform pan. Bake at 350 degrees for 6 minutes. Remove from the oven and cool. Spread 1/2 of the caramel sauce over the crust and freeze. Spread the chocolate ice cream over the caramel sauce and freeze. Combine the vanilla ice cream and toffee candy in a bowl. Spread over the chocolate ice cream and freeze. Spread 1/2 the chocolate sauce over the chocolate ice cream, leaving a 1 inch border and freeze. Spread the coffee ice cream over the chocolate sauce and freeze. Remove the dessert from the freezer 10 minutes before serving. Cut into slices. Drizzle with the remaining caramel sauce and chocolate sauce.

Serves 12 to 14

SHORELINE
Michigan has over 120 lighthouses located throughout the Lower and Upper Peninsulas— more than any other state. In addition, if you count the islands of our great state, you can walk 3,126 miles of shoreline, which means the state has more sugary sand than all the Caribbean islands combined.

Frozen Oreo Dessert

25	Oreo cookies, crushed
1/3	cup margarine, melted
1/2	gallon vanilla ice cream, softened
4	ounces semisweet chocolate
1	cup confectioners' sugar
2	tablespoons butter
1	(5-ounce) can evaporated milk

Combine the Oreos and margarine in a bowl. Pat into a greased 9×13-inch baking pan and freeze. Spread the ice cream over the Oreo layer and freeze. Melt the chocolate in a saucepan over very low heat. Add the sugar, butter and evaporated milk. Cook until thickened, stirring constantly; set aside until cool. Spread the chocolate sauce over the ice cream. Freeze until ready to serve.

Serves 32

Lemon Ice

4	cups milk
2	cups sugar
	Grated zest of 2 lemons
1	cup heavy cream
3/4	cup lemon juice

Scald the milk, sugar and lemon zest in a saucepan. Cool. Add the cream and lemon juice. Pour into an ice cream freezer container. Freeze for 16 minutes using the manufacturer's directions. Spoon into a freezer container. Freeze until firm.

Serves 10

PEACHES

When shopping for peaches, look for fruit that are free from bruises and decay, and be sure they have that wonderful "peach" smell. Peaches should not be too soft or overripe. Michigan ranks fourth in the nation in peach production. Michigan's "Red Haven" peaches are famous throughout the country and have become the most widely planted variety in the world.

Between the Lakes

Fresh Peach Cobbler

1/2   cup (1 stick) butter,
      at room temperature
1/2   cup sugar
1   cup flour
2   teaspoons baking powder
1/4   teaspoon salt
1/2   cup milk
6   cups sliced peeled peaches
1/2   cup packed brown sugar
1   teaspoon vanilla extract
1   teaspoon cinnamon
1 1/2 tablespoons cornstarch
2   tablespoons butter

Cut 1/2 cup butter into pieces. Combine with the sugar in a food processor fitted with a steel blade and process until smooth or cream together in a mixing bowl. Add the flour, baking powder, salt and milk. Pulse 4 or 5 times until combined; the batter will be stiff. Set aside. Combine the peaches, brown sugar, vanilla, cinnamon and cornstarch in a large bowl and toss gently to mix. Pour the peach mixture into a buttered 7x11-inch baking dish. Dot with 2 tablespoons butter. Spoon the batter over the peaches, covering most of the fruit. Bake at 350 degrees for 40 to 50 minutes or until the pastry is golden and the peaches are bubbling. Serve warm with ice cream.

Serves 6

Raspberry Soufflé

4   (10-ounce) packages frozen
      raspberries, or 3 pints fresh
      raspberries
1/4   cup kirsch or almond liqueur
6   ladyfingers, diced
2   tablespoons kirsch
1   cup sugar
1/4   cup water
1/2   teaspoon cream of tarter
5   egg whites, at room temperature
1   cup whipping cream, whipped
2   tablespoons chopped pistachios

Purée the raspberries in a blender. Add 1/4 cup kirsch and mix well. Sprinkle the ladyfingers with 2 tablespoons kirsch; set aside. Combine the sugar, water and cream of tartar in a saucepan. Cook, uncovered, over medium heat to 234 to 240 degrees on a candy thermometer, soft-ball stage.

Beat the egg whites in a mixing bowl until soft peaks form. Slowly pour the hot sugar syrup into the egg whites while beating. Gradually add the raspberry purée. Fold in the whipped cream. Pour 1/2 the raspberry mixture into a 1-quart mold. Add the ladyfingers and top with the remaining raspberry mixture. Sprinkle with the pistachios. Freeze until firm. Remove from the freezer 5 minutes before serving.

Note: You may substitute cherries for the raspberries.

Serves 10 to 12

Strawberry Shortcake Dessert

12   Twinkies
2   quarts strawberries
1/2   cup sugar
16   ounces whipped topping

Slice the Twinkies lengthwise into halves. Place the Twinkies filling side up in a single layer in a 9×13-inch baking dish. Slice the strawberries and place in a bowl. Sprinkle with the sugar. Spread the strawberries over the Twinkies. Spread the whipped topping over the strawberries. Chill, covered, 8 to 12 hours.

Serves 12

Summer Trifle Cake

2   (4-ounce) packages instant vanilla pudding
3   cups milk
1   package red pie glaze
2   angel food cakes, torn into bite-size pieces
16   ounces whipped topping
6   to 8 cups bite-size fruit of choice: strawberries, blueberries, raspberries or any summer fruit

Prepare the pudding according to the package directions using the milk; set aside. Spread a thin layer of pie glaze on the bottom of a large glass bowl. Layer half the angel food cake, pudding and whipped topping in the bowl. Add a thin layer of pie glaze. Top with the fruit. Repeat the layers of the angel food cake, pudding, whipped topping and fruit. Chill, covered, for 8 to 12 hours before serving.

Serves 20

Between the Lakes

Caramel and Banana Sauce

1	cup packed brown sugar
1/4	cup milk
2	tablespoons butter
1	teaspoon vanilla extract
1	banana, mashed
2	tablespoons raisins, or more to taste
2	tablespoons rum, or more to taste
	Nuts (optional)

Combine the brown sugar, milk, butter and vanilla extract in a saucepan. Bring to a boil and stir until smooth. Add the banana, raisins, rum and nuts. Serve over vanilla ice cream.

Serves 6

Da's Famous Fudge Sauce

8	ounces semisweet chocolate
2	cups cream or milk
1/2	cup (1 stick) butter
3	to 4 cups sugar
3	to 4 tablespoons vanilla extract
	Nuts (optional)

Combine the chocolate and cream in a saucepan. Cook over medium heat, stirring constantly. Add the butter, stirring until the chocolate melts. Add the sugar. Boil for 5 minutes stirring constantly. Remove from the heat. Add the vanilla and nuts and stir. Serve over ice cream.

Serves about 32

Fresh Apple Cake with Caramel Glaze

2	cups sugar	1/2	teaspoon mace
1 1/2	cups vegetable oil	1/2	teaspoon salt
3	eggs	3	cups diced apples
2	teaspoons vanilla extract		Juice of 1 lemon
3	cups flour	1	cup chopped walnuts
2	teaspoons cinnamon		Caramel Glaze
1	teaspoon baking soda		(see below)

Beat the sugar and oil in a mixing bowl until smooth. Add the eggs 1 at a time, beating well after each addition. Add the vanilla. Stir the flour, cinnamon, baking soda, mace and salt together in a bowl. Gradually add to the egg mixture, beating constantly. Place the apples in a bowl and sprinkle with lemon juice. Fold the apples into the batter. Add the walnuts. The batter will be very thick. Spoon into a well greased and floured bundt pan. Bake at 325 degrees for 1 1/4 hours. Remove from the oven and cool on a wire rack for 15 minutes. Invert onto a serving plate and cool on the rack. Spoon the Caramel Glaze over the cooled cake.

Serves 16

Caramel Glaze

6   tablespoons butter
6   tablespoons brown sugar
1/4 cup heavy cream
1   teaspoon vanilla extract

Melt the butter in a small saucepan. Add the brown sugar, cream and vanilla. Bring to a rolling boil. Boil rapidly for 3 to 4 minutes or until the mixture sheets off a spoon. Cool slightly.

Apple Cider Pound Cake

3	cups sugar		1/2	teaspoon allspice
1 1/2	cups (3 sticks) butter or margarine, softened		1/2	teaspoon nutmeg
			1/4	teaspoon ground cloves
6	eggs		1	cup apple cider
3	cups flour		1	teaspoon vanilla extract
1/2	teaspoon salt			Buttermilk Icing
1/2	teaspoon baking powder			(see below)
1	teaspoon cinnamon			

Cream the sugar and butter in a large mixing bowl until light and fluffy. Add the eggs 1 at a time, beating well after each addition. Combine the flour, salt, baking powder, cinnamon, allspice, nutmeg and cloves. Set aside. Combine the cider and vanilla. Add the dry ingredients alternately with the cider to the creamed mixture, mixing well after each addition. Spoon into a greased and sugared (with granulated sugar) 10-inch tube pan or bundt pan. Bake at 325 degrees for 1 1/2 hours or until the cake tests done. Cool the cake in the pan; invert onto a serving plate. Drizzle the Buttermilk Icing over each cake slice just before serving.

Serves 12 to 16

Buttermilk Icing

1/2   cup sugar
1/4   cup (1/2 stick) butter or margarine
1/4   cup buttermilk
1/2   teaspoon vanilla extract
1/4   teaspoon baking soda

Combine the sugar, butter, buttermilk, vanilla and baking soda in a saucepan. Bring to a boil. Reduce the heat and simmer for 10 minutes.

Brown Sugar Pound Cake

1   (1-pound) package light brown sugar
1   cup sugar
1   cup vegetable shortening
1/2 cup (1 stick) butter or margarine
5   eggs
1   teaspoon vanilla extract
3   tablespoons butternut and
      vanilla flavoring
3   cups flour
1   teaspoon baking powder
1/2 teaspoon salt
1   cup milk
1   cup nuts (optional)

Cream the brown sugar, sugar, shortening and butter in a large mixing bowl until light and fluffy. Add the eggs 1 at a time, beating well after each addition Add the vanilla and butternut and vanilla flavoring, mixing well. Combine the flour, baking powder and salt in a bowl. Add the dry ingredients alternately with the milk to the creamed mixture, mixing well after each addition. Stir in the nuts. Spoon into a greased and sugared (with granulated sugar) 10-inch tube pan. Bake at 325 degrees for 1 1/2 hours. Cool the cake in the pan; invert onto a serving plate.

Serves 16

Banana Birthday Cake

1 1/2 cups sugar
1/2   cup (1 stick) butter, softened
3   eggs
1/4   cup sour milk
1 1/2 teaspoons baking soda
1/2   teaspoon baking powder
1 1/2 cups flour
3   ripe bananas, mashed
1   teaspoon vanilla extract
1   cup chopped nuts (optional)
        Chocolate buttercream frosting

Cream the sugar and butter in a large mixing bowl until light and fluffy. Add the eggs, one at a time, beating well after each addition. Beat in the sour milk, baking soda, baking powder and flour. Add the bananas, vanilla and nuts. Pour into 2 floured 8-inch cake pans. Bake at 350 degrees for 30 minutes. Fill and frost with your favorite chocolate buttercream frosting.

Serves 8 to 10

Between the Lakes

Chocolate Chocolate Chip Cake

2   cups sour cream
2   eggs
1/2   cup Kahlúa
1   (2-layer) package devil's food or other cake mix without
      pudding
1   (4-ounce) package chocolate pudding mix
1/4   cup vegetable oil
2   cups (12 ounces) semisweet chocolate chips
      Confectioners' sugar for sprinkling

Combine the sour cream, eggs, Kahlúa, cake mix, pudding mix and oil in a large mixing bowl and mix well. Stir in the chocolate chips. Pour into a bundt pan. Bake at 350 degrees for 45 to 50 minutes or until the cake springs back when lightly touched. Cool in the pan. Invert onto a serving plate and sprinkle with the confectioners' sugar.

Serves 16

The Greatest Carrot Cake

2   cups flour
1   teaspoon baking soda
2   teaspoons cinnamon
1   teaspoon salt
2   cups sugar
1 1/2   cups vegetable oil
3   eggs
1   cup crushed pineapple, well drained
2   cups finely grated carrots
1   cup shredded coconut
1   cup chopped walnuts
1   teaspoon vanilla extract
     Cream Cheese Frosting (see below)

Sift the flour, baking soda, cinnamon and salt into a mixing bowl. Set aside. Beat the sugar, oil and eggs together in a mixing bowl. Gradually add the flour mixture. Fold in the pineapple, carrots, coconut and walnuts. Stir in the vanilla. Pour into a greased 9×13-inch cake pan. Bake at 350 degrees for 1 hour. Remove from the oven and cool. Spread with the Cream Cheese Frosting.

Serves 12 to 15

Cream Cheese Frosting

1   (8-ounce) package cream cheese, softened
1/2   cup (1 stick) butter, softened
2   teaspoons vanilla extract
4   cups sifted confectioners' sugar

Beat the cream cheese, butter and vanilla in a large mixing bowl. Gradually add the confectioners' sugar, beating until smooth.

Milky Way Swirl Cake

2¹/₂	(2.05-ounce) Milky Way bars, sliced	¹/₂	cup (1 stick) butter, melted
2	tablespoons water	3	eggs
1	(2-layer) package yellow cake mix with pudding	1	tablespoon flour
1	cup water		Milky Way Glaze (see below)

Place the Milky Way bars and 2 tablespoons water in a saucepan. Melt over low heat, stirring until the mixture is smooth. Remove from the heat and set aside. Beat the cake mix, 1 cup water, melted butter and eggs at low speed in a mixing bowl for 1 minute. Scrape down the sides of the bowl. Increase the speed to medium and beat for 2 minutes longer. Measure out ²/₃ cup batter and stir into the melted Milky Way mixture. Add the flour and stir until smooth; set aside. Pour the plain batter into a lightly greased and floured 12-cup bundt pan. Spoon on the Milky Way mixture in a ring. Do not touch the sides of the pan. Swirl through the batter with a knife and smooth the top with a spatula. Bake at 325 degrees for 45 to 50 minutes or until the cake springs back when lightly touched and starts to pull away from the side of the pan. Remove from the oven. Place on a wire rack and cool for 20 minutes. Run a sharp knife around the edge of the cake and invert onto a wire rack. Cool completely. Slide the cake onto a serving plate. Spoon the Milky Way Glaze over the cake to drip down the sides. Let stand for 10 minutes.

Serves 16

Milky Way Glaze

2¹/₂	(2.05-ounce) Milky Way bars, sliced	2	tablespoons butter
		2	teaspoons water

Place the Milky Way bars in a saucepan over medium-low heat. Add the butter and water. Cook until smooth, stirring constantly. Cool the glaze for 10 minutes.

Orange Pour-Over Cake

1	cup shortening	1	cup buttermilk
1 1/4	cups sugar	1	teaspoon vanilla extract
3	medium eggs	1	cup chopped walnuts
2 1/2	cups flour	1	cup chopped dates
2	teaspoons baking powder		Grated zest of 2 oranges
1	teaspoon baking soda		Orange Syrup Glaze
1	teaspoon salt		(see below)

Cream the shortening in a large mixing bowl. Add the sugar gradually and cream until light and fluffy. Add the eggs 1 at a time, beating well after each addition. Sift the flour, baking powder, baking soda and salt into a bowl. Add to the creamed mixture alternately with the buttermilk, mixing well after each addition. Fold in the vanilla, walnuts, dates and orange zest. Pour into a well-greased 3-inch-deep springform pan. Bake at 375 degrees for 1 hour. Cool for 10 minutes. Perforate the cake using a wooden pick. Pour the warm Orange Syrup Glaze over the cake. Let stand for several hours.

Serves 16

Orange Syrup Glaze

3	oranges, peeled
1 1/2	cups sugar

Squeeze the juice and pulp from the oranges into a saucepan. Add the sugar. Bring to a boil. Reduce the heat and simmer until the sugar dissolves and the mixture becomes transparent.

Do-Nothing Pineapple Cake

2   cups flour
2   cups sugar
1   teaspoon baking soda
1/2   teaspoon salt
1   (20-ounce) can crushed pineapple
2   eggs
1   teaspoon vanilla extract
    Pecan Icing (see below)

Combine the flour, sugar, baking soda and salt in a large bowl and mix well. Stir in the pineapple, eggs and vanilla. Pour into a greased and lightly floured 9×13-inch cake pan. Bake at 350 degrees for 30 to 40 minutes. Pour the Pecan Icing over the hot cake.

Serves 15

Pecan Icing

1/2   cup (1 stick) margarine
1   (5-ounce) can evaporated milk
1   cup sugar
1   cup chopped pecans or walnuts
1   cup shredded coconut (optional)

Combine the margarine, evaporated milk and sugar in a saucepan. Bring to a boil and cook for 5 minutes, stirring constantly. Remove from the heat. Stir in the pecans and coconut.

SUGAR
The sugar beet industry has a century-long history of success in Michigan. Sugar from sugar beets is identical in chemical formula, nutritional value, taste, appearance and sweetening powers to cane sugar. Sugar is nature's sweetener and has only 15 calories per teaspoon. It takes 12 beets to make one pound of sugar.

Pumpkin Cake Roll

3	eggs	1/2	teaspoon nutmeg
1	cup sugar	1/2	teaspoon salt
2/3	cup canned pumpkin	1	cup finely chopped
1	teaspoon lemon juice		walnuts
3/4	cup flour		Confectioners' sugar for
1	teaspoon baking powder		sprinkling
2	teaspoons cinnamon		Cream Cheese Filling
1	teaspoon ginger		(see below)

Beat the eggs at high speed in a mixing bowl for 5 minutes. Gradually beat in the sugar. Stir in the pumpkin and lemon juice. Sift the flour, baking powder, cinnamon, ginger, nutmeg and salt into a bowl. Fold into the pumpkin mixture. Spread in a greased and floured 10×15-inch cake pan. Sprinkle with the walnuts. Bake at 375 degrees for 15 minutes. Remove from the oven. Dust a clean kitchen towel with confectioners' sugar. Invert the cake onto the towel. Roll the warm cake in the towel as for a jelly roll from the short side and place on a wire rack to cool. Unroll the cooled cake carefully and remove the towel. Spread the Cream Cheese Filling within 1 inch of the edge and reroll. Chill, covered, in the refrigerator. Sprinkle with confectioners' sugar before serving.

Serves 8

Cream Cheese Filling

1	cup confectioners' sugar
2	(3-ounce) packages cream cheese, softened
1/4	cup (1/2 stick) butter, softened
1/2	teaspoon vanilla extract

Beat the confectioners' sugar, cream cheese, butter and vanilla in a large bowl until smooth.

Best-Ever Rhubarb Cake

1 1/2   cups packed brown sugar
1/2   cup shortening
1   cup buttermilk
1   egg
1   teaspoon vanilla extract
2   cups flour
1   teaspoon baking soda
1 1/2   cups finely diced rhubarb
1/4   cup sugar
1 1/2   teaspoons cinnamon

Cream the brown sugar and shortening in a large mixing bowl until light and fluffy. Add the buttermilk, egg and vanilla and mix well. Add the flour and baking soda and mix well. Fold in the rhubarb. Spoon into a greased 9×13-inch cake pan. Combine the sugar and cinnamon in a small bowl. Sprinkle over the batter. Bake at 350 degrees for 40 minutes.

Serves 15

Rum Cake

1	cup yellow cake mix
1	(4-ounce) package vanilla instant pudding mix
4	eggs
1/2	cup cold water
1/2	cup vegetable oil
1/2	cup dark rum
1	cup chopped pecans
	Rum Glaze (see below)

Combine the cake mix, pudding mix, eggs, cold water, oil and rum in a large mixing bowl. Beat for 3 minutes. Sprinkle the pecans in the bottom of a greased and floured bundt pan. Pour the batter over the pecans. Bake at 325 degrees on the middle rack of the oven for 1 hour. Cool for 10 minutes; invert onto a wire rack. Drizzle the Rum Glaze over the cake.

Serves 16

Rum Glaze

1/2	cup (1 stick) butter
1/4	cup water
1	cup sugar
1/2	cup dark rum

Melt the butter in a medium saucepan. Add the water and sugar. Boil for 5 minutes, stirring constantly. Remove from the heat. Stir in the rum.

Between the Lakes

Strawberry Treasure Cake

2 cups cake flour	1 cup minus
1 tablespoon baking	2 tablespoons milk
powder	1½ teaspoons vanilla extract
1 teaspoon salt	Meringue Frosting
1⅓ cups sugar	(see below)
½ cup shortening	1½ quarts strawberries
2 eggs	

Sift the cake flour, baking powder, salt and sugar into a large mixing bowl. Add the shortening, eggs, milk and vanilla. Beat for 3 minutes or 200 strokes. Pour into two 9-inch cake pans lined with greased and floured parchment paper. Bake at 375 degrees for 30 minutes. Cool in the pans for 10 minutes. Invert onto a wire rack to cool completely. Spread a layer of Meringue Frosting on 1 cake layer. Slice enough strawberries to cover the surface and arrange over the layer. Add the remaining cake layer. Frost the top and side of the cake. Decorate with the remaining whole strawberries.

Serves 8

Meringue Frosting

½ cup water	3 tablespoons sugar
1½ cups sugar	1 teaspoon vanilla extract
1 teaspoon light corn	1 or 2 drops red food
syrup	coloring
3 egg whites, at room	
temperature	

Combine the water, 1½ cups sugar and corn syrup in a saucepan. Boil the sugar syrup for 10 minutes or until it spins a medium thread. Beat the egg whites with 3 tablespoons sugar in a mixing bowl until stiff peaks form. Gradually add the sugar syrup. Beat until stiff. Add the vanilla and food coloring.

Michigan Nut and Berry Bark

1   pound bittersweet chocolate,
     finely chopped
1   cup nuts, toasted (such as almonds,
     walnuts or macadamia)
1   cup dried cranberries, apricots
     or cherries
1/4 cup flaked coconut, toasted
1/2 cup dried cranberries, apricots
     or cherries
1/2 cup nuts, toasted
1/4 cup flaked coconut, toasted
4   ounces white chocolate, melted

Melt bittersweet chocolate in the top of a double boiler over simmering water. Stir in 1 cup nuts, 1 cup dried cranberries and 1/4 cup coconut. Pour onto a parchment- or foil-lined 10×15-inch baking pan. Spread the chocolate mixture over the parchment to a 10×14-inch rectangle with a rubber spatula. Sprinkle with 1/2 cup dried cranberries, 1/2 cup nuts and 1/4 cup coconut. Cover with plastic wrap and gently pat down. Remove the plastic wrap and drizzle with the white chocolate. Chill, covered, until the bark is hard. Break into large pieces. Store in an airtight container for a week or freeze in sealable plastic bags.

Serves 14

Peanut Butter Crunch Bars

2   cups peanut butter
1   cup light corn syrup
1   cup sugar
6   cups Special K cereal
2   cups (12 ounces) semisweet
     chocolate chips

Combine the peanut butter, corn syrup and sugar in a saucepan. Heat and stir to blend. Stir in the cereal gradually. Press the peanut butter mixture into a 9×13-inch baking pan. Sprinkle with chocolate chips. Place the pan in a warm oven to melt the chocolate chips. Remove when the chocolate chips are soft. Spread the chips with a spatula. Cool until the chocolate firms up.

Serves 15

Between the Lakes

Animal Cookies

3/4 cup sugar
1 cup (2 sticks) butter, softened
1 egg
1/2 teaspoon salt
2 tablespoons sour cream
1 1/2 cups flour
1 teaspoon vanilla extract
1 egg white
1 tablespoon water
3 to 4 cups confectioners' sugar

Cream the sugar and butter in a mixing bowl until light and fluffy. Add the egg, salt, sour cream, flour and vanilla and mix well. Chill, covered, for several hours. Roll the dough 1/8 to 1/4 inch thick on a floured surface. Cut with animal-shaped cookie cutters. Place on a nonstick cookie sheet. Bake at 350 degrees for 6 to 8 minutes or until the cookies just start to brown. Cool on the cookie sheet for 2 minutes. Remove to a wire rack to cool completely. Combine the egg white, water and enough confectioners' sugar to make a frosting in a large bowl and mix well. Spread over the cookies.

Makes about 1 dozen cookies

MACKINAC ISLAND FUDGE

A candy maker moved to Mackinac (pronounced "Mackinaw") Island in 1887 to work at the famous Grand Hotel. One day a mistake was made in a chocolate fondant preparation, causing it to set up on the marble slab. The result was "fudge" with a smooth, creamy texture, never before experienced. This encouraged the candy maker to develop and refine this creaming technique to form fudge unsurpassed in excellence to this day.

Disappearing Marshmallow Brownies

6   ounces butterscotch chips
1/4 cup (1/2 stick) butter
3/4 cup flour
1/3 cup firmly packed brown sugar
1   teaspoon baking powder
1/4 teaspoon salt
1/2 teaspoon vanilla extract
1   egg
1   cup marshmallows
1   cup (6 ounces) semisweet
     chocolate chips

Melt the butterscotch chips and butter in a heavy saucepan, stirring constantly. Cool to lukewarm. Add the flour, brown sugar, baking powder, salt, vanilla and egg and mix well. Fold in the marshmallows and chocolate chips. Spread in a greased 9×9-inch baking pan. Bake at 350 degrees for 20 to 25 minutes. The center will be soft but firms up when cool. Do not overbake.

Serves 12

Chocolate Caramel Bars

50   vanilla caramels, unwrapped
1/3 cup evaporated milk
1   (2-layer) package German chocolate
     cake mix
1/2 cup (1 stick) margarine
1   cup chopped nuts
1/3 cup evaporated milk
1   cup (6 ounces) milk chocolate chips
     Vanilla ice cream (optional)

Melt the caramels and 1/3 cup evaporated milk in a heavy saucepan. Set aside. Combine the cake mix, margarine, nuts and 1/3 cup evaporated milk in a mixing bowl and mix well. Pat 2/3 of the chocolate cake mixture into a 9×13-inch baking pan. Bake at 350 degrees for 6 minutes. Remove from the oven. Sprinkle with the chocolate chips. Pour on the caramel sauce. Sprinkle with the remaining chocolate cake mixture. Bake at 350 degrees for 15 to 18 minutes. Serve topped with ice cream.

Serves 15

Between the Lakes

Crème de Menthe Squares

1/2   cup (1 stick) butter
1/2   cup baking cocoa
1/2   cup confectioners' sugar
1   egg, beaten
1   teaspoon vanilla extract
2   cups graham cracker crumbs
1/2   cup (1 stick) butter
1/3   cup green crème de menthe
3   cups confectioners' sugar
1/4   cup (1/2 stick) butter
1 1/2 cups (9 ounces) semisweet
      chocolate chips

Combine 1/2 cup butter and the baking cocoa in a saucepan. Heat until the butter melts, stirring frequently. Remove from the heat. Stir in 1/2 cup confectioners' sugar, the egg and vanilla. Stir in the graham cracker crumbs. Press in the bottom of a 9×13-inch baking pan lightly sprayed with nonstick baking spray. Set aside. Melt 1/2 cup butter in a small saucepan. Pour into a mixing bowl. Add the crème de menthe. Beat in 3 cups confectioners' sugar at low speed until smooth. Spread the crème de menthe mixture over the graham cracker layer. Chill for 30 minutes. Melt 1/4 cup butter and the chocolate chips in a saucepan over low heat. Spread the chocolate over the crème de menthe layer. Chill, covered, for 1 to 2 hours. Cut into small squares.

Serves 30

Cream Cheese Cookies

1/2   cup (1 stick) butter, softened
1   (3-ounce) package cream cheese,
      softened
1   cup sugar
1 1/4 cups flour
1/2   cup chopped walnuts or pecans
      Sugar for dipping
      Colored frosting

Cream the butter, cream cheese and 1 cup sugar in a mixing bowl until light and fluffy. Add the flour by hand, mixing well. Stir in the walnuts. Drop by tablespoonfuls onto an ungreased cookie sheet. Flatten the cookies with a glass dipped in sugar. Bake at 375 degrees for 8 to 10 minutes. Cool on the cookie sheet for 3 minutes. Remove the cookies to a wire rack to cool completely. Drizzle with colored frosting.

Makes about 2 dozen cookies

Lemon Cheese Logs

1   cup sugar
1   cup (2 sticks) butter, softened
1   (3-ounce) package cream cheese,
     softened
1   egg yolk
2 1/2 cups flour
1   cup finely chopped walnuts
1/2 teaspoon salt
1/2 teaspoon grated lemon zest
1   cup (6 ounces) semisweet
     chocolate chips
     Colored sugar (optional)

Cream the sugar, butter and cream
cheese in a mixing bowl until light and
fluffy. Beat in the egg yolk. Stir in the flour,
walnuts, salt and lemon zest and mix well.
Chill, covered, for at least 1 hour. Shape
the dough by teaspoonfuls into 2-inch logs.
Place on an ungreased cookie sheet. Bake
at 325 degrees for 12 minutes. Remove
from the oven and cool. Melt the chocolate
chips. Dip one end of each cookie in the
melted chocolate. Let partially set, then dip
in colored sugar. Place on a wire rack until
the chocolate is firm.

Makes about 3 1/2 dozen cookies

Lemon Bars

2   cups flour
3/4 cup confectioners' sugar
1   cup (2 sticks) butter or margarine
2   cups sugar
1/4 cup flour
4   to 6 tablespoons lemon juice
4   eggs, beaten
     Confectioners' sugar

Combine 2 cups flour and 3/4 cup
confectioners' sugar in a large bowl. Cut
in the butter until crumbly. Pat into a
9×13-inch baking pan. Bake at 350 degrees
for 15 minutes. Remove from the oven.
Combine the sugar, 1/4 cup flour, lemon
juice and eggs in a mixing bowl and mix
well. Spread over the baked layer. Bake for
25 minutes longer. Remove from the oven
and sprinkle with confectioners' sugar. Cool
and cut into bars.

Serves 15

Between the Lakes

Maple Cookies

1/2 cup shortening
1 cup packed brown sugar
1/2 cup sugar
2 eggs
1 cup sour cream or fat-free sour cream
1 teaspoon maple flavoring
2 3/4 cups flour
1/2 teaspoon baking soda
1 teaspoon salt
Maple Frosting (see below)

Beat the shortening, brown sugar, sugar and eggs in a mixing bowl until light and fluffy. Add the sour cream and beat until blended. Mix in the maple flavoring, flour, baking soda and salt. Drop by teaspoonfuls onto a nonstick cookie sheet. Bake at 375 degrees for 10 minutes or until the cookies are lightly browned at the edges and spring back when lightly touched. Remove from the oven. Remove the cookies to a wire rack to cool completely. Spread with Maple Frosting.

Makes 4 to 6 dozen cookies

Maple Frosting

1/4 cup (1/2 stick) butter or margarine, softened
1/2 teaspoon salt
2 teaspoons maple flavoring
3 cups confectioners' sugar
1/4 cup milk

Cream the butter in a mixing bowl until light and fluffy. Add the salt and maple flavoring and mix well. Add the confectioners' sugar and milk alternately, mixing well after each addition.

Molasses Cookies

1 1/2 cups melted shortening
2 cups sugar
1/2 cup molasses
2 eggs
4 cups flour
4 teaspoons baking soda
1 teaspoon ground cloves
1 teaspoon ginger
1 tablespoon cinnamon
1 teaspoon salt
Sugar for rolling

Beat the shortening and 2 cups sugar in a mixing bowl until light and fluffy. Add the molasses and eggs and mix well. Stir the flour, baking soda, cloves, ginger, cinnamon and salt together in a bowl. Add the dry ingredients to the shortening mixture and mix well. Shape the dough into balls and roll in sugar. Place on a nonstick cookie sheet. Bake at 350 degrees for 8 to 10 minutes. Do not overbake.

Makes about 4 dozen cookies

Pecan Pie Bars

1 (2-layer) package yellow cake mix
1/2 cup (1 stick) butter or margarine, melted
1 egg or equivalent egg substitute
1/2 cup packed brown sugar
1 1/2 cups dark corn syrup
1 teaspoon vanilla extract
3 eggs or equivalent egg substitute
2 cups chopped pecans

Set aside 2/3 cup cake mix. Combine the remaining cake mix, butter and 1 egg in a mixing bowl and mix well. Press on the bottom and sides of a well-greased 9×13-inch baking pan. Bake at 350 degrees for 15 to 20 minutes or until light brown. Beat the reserved cake mix, brown sugar, corn syrup, vanilla and 3 eggs at medium speed in a mixing bowl for 1 to 2 minutes. Spread over the baked layer. Sprinkle with the pecans. Bake for 30 to 35 minutes longer or until the filling is set. Cool before cutting.

Makes about 1 1/2 dozen bars

Between the Lakes

Potato Chip Cookies

1	cup shortening
1	cup packed brown sugar
1	cup sugar
2	eggs, beaten
2 1/2	cups flour
1	teaspoon baking soda
2	cups crushed potato chips
1	cup (6 ounces) butterscotch chips

Cream the shortening, brown sugar and sugar in a mixing bowl until light and fluffy. Add the eggs and beat well. Mix in the flour and baking soda. Add the potato chips and butterscotch chips. Shape into balls the size of walnuts. Place on an ungreased cookie sheet. Bake at 325 degrees for 15 minutes.

Makes about 4 dozen cookies

Located on a wooded campus just 16 miles southwest of Traverse City, Interlochen Arts Camp is one of the oldest and most successful fine arts camps in the world. In the 2001-2002 year Interlochen played host to students from 24 countries creating an amazingly diverse international environment in which students have the opportunity to hone their talents.

Sour Cream Cookies

1	cup sugar
1/2	cup (1 stick) butter, softened
1/2	cup lard
1	teaspoon baking soda
1	cup sour cream
1	egg
1	teaspoon baking powder
2	cups flour
1/2	teaspoon nutmeg
	Pinch of salt
	Sugar for sprinkling

Mix 1 cup sugar, butter and lard in a large mixing bowl. Combine the baking soda and sour cream in a bowl and stir into the sugar mixture. Add the egg. Combine the baking powder and flour and stir into the sugar mixture. Add the nutmeg and salt and mix well. Chill, covered, for 1 to 2 hours. Pat the dough out on a lightly floured surface to 1/2 inch thickness. Cut with a cookie cutter. Sprinkle with sugar. Place on a greased cookie sheet. Bake at 350 degrees for 10 minutes.

Makes about 2 dozen cookies

Between the Lakes

Index

Between the Lakes

Between the Lakes

Between the Lakes

Between the Lakes
A Collection of Michigan Recipes

**MAIL ORDER
FORM TO**

Junior League
of Saginaw Valley
c/o Cookbook
Committee
5228 State Street
Saginaw,
Michigan 48603
989-790-3763

	QTY	AMT DUE
Between the Lakes at $22.95 per book	_____	$ _____
Shipping and Handling $4.00 for first book, $2.00 for each additonal book		$ _____
Subtotal		$ _____
Sales Tax 6% for Michigan residents		$ _____
TOTAL		$ _____

Please make check payable to Junior League of Saginaw Valley.

Sold to: *(Please print)*

Name _____

Address _____

City _____ State _____ Zip _____

Telephone _____ E-mail _____

Ship to: *(if different from above)*

Name _____

Address _____

City _____ State _____ Zip _____

Telephone _____

Photocopies of this form will be accepted.